potatoes

from gnocchi to mash

potatoes

from gnocchi to mash

Annie Nichols

photography by Peter Myers

RYLAND
PETERS
& SMALL

Creative Director **Jacqui Small**

Art Editor **Penny Stock**

Designer **Lucy Hamilton**

Editor **Elsa Petersen-Schepelern**

Photography **Peter Myers**

Food Stylist **Annie Nichols**

Stylist **Wei Tang**

Indexer **Hilary Bird**

Production **Kate Mackillop**

Author Photograph **Catherine Rowlands**

Dedication

To Winnie and Fred Nichols, my mum and dad, for a
childhood full of wholesome food, especially Dad's
new potatoes – the best in the west.

My thanks to Dave and Allan, Pete and Sean Myers,
Wei Tang, the gang at Backgrounds and to Becky
Johnson for her enthusiastic assistance. Thanks also to
Marwan Badran, his mother Leonora and his aunt
Rainie for their generous help with the Iraqi recipes.

Notes

All potatoes and other vegetables are washed then
peeled in the usual way, unless otherwise noted.
Where relevant, a particular kind of potato is
specified in the recipes, such as floury or waxy.
See page 6 for suitable varieties. Where the kind
of potato is not specified, use either variety.
Ovens should be preheated to the specified
temperature. If using a fan oven, cooking times should
be reduced according to manufacturer's instructions.

Hardcover edition first published in the United Kingdom in
1998. Paperback edition first published in the United Kingdom
in 1999 by Ryland Peters & Small
Cavendish House, 51–55 Mortimer Street, London WIN 7TD

Text © Annie Nichols 1998
Design and photographs © Ryland Peters & Small 1998
10 9 8 7 6 5 4 3 2

Printed and bound in China by Toppan Printing Co.

Hardcover ISBN 1 900518 57 0
Paperback ISBN 1 900518 93 7

A CIP record for this book is available from the British Library.

contents

There are hundreds of different varieties of potatoes, and each country has developed breeds suitable for their own climatic and market conditions. However, all these varieties can be divided into just a few categories, based on their suitability for different culinary uses.

Waxy varieties (centre) which are grown in Britain, include new and Early potatoes such as Pentland Javelin, Nadine, Arran Comet, Ulster Prince and Concorde. These are suitable for boiling and serving whole in salads. Other waxy potatoes include Marfona and the red-skinned Maincrop, Desirée.

Floury varieties (far right) are best for mashing, baking, roasting and deep-frying, and include the Maincrops Maris Piper, King Edward, Fianna, Golden Wonder, Cara and Morene.

New potatoes, with their thin, flaky skins, should be used within a few days of purchase. Varieties include Colmo, Maris Bard, Duke of York, Dundrod and the famous Jersey Royals.

Speciality salad potatoes include Charlotte, La Ratte, Pink Fir Apple, Linzer Delicatess, Anya, Belle de Fontenay and the blue, black and purple potatoes such as Shetland Blacks, Edzell Blues and Purple Congos. All are wonderful simply boiled and tossed in butter, chopped herbs and seasonings. Cooking blue potatoes in a microwave oven helps preserve their colour.

potato varieties

boiled and steamed
potatoes

Mashed potatoes, salads and crushes

Boiling and Steaming Potatoes

New potatoes should be added to salted boiling water – old potatoes put in cold salted water then brought to the boil. Steaming takes a little longer than boiling. Boil or steam similar-sized potatoes together to make sure they cook evenly. Don't test for tenderness until towards the end of cooking time, or the potatoes will absorb water, become soggy and fall apart. Most of the nutrients are just under the skin of the potato, so leave the skin on when boiling, and peel only when cooked. Peeled potatoes also absorb more water. Take care peeling hot potatoes – hold them in a clean cloth, or leave until cool enough to handle, then reheat as necessary.

Mashed Potatoes

Soft, fluffy and creamy – mashed potato is the epitome of comfort food. It can be served as a side dish, as a dish in its own right, or used as the basis for many other dishes, such as croquettes or potato cakes. People like different kinds of mashed potato – from coarse and lumpy, to light and fluffy, or an almost pourable consistency. Choose floury potatoes for the best textured mashed potatoes. Waxy potatoes produce a lumpy mash, known as a crush. Potatoes cooked in their skins retain nutrients and have a dry texture which takes liquids and flavourings better. If boiling peeled chunks of potato, drain when cooked, return to the pan, and allow to steam dry for a few minutes. Mash with a potato masher for a coarse texture, or press through a food mill (mouli de légumes – see page 96) for a fluffy, light texture. A good result can also be achieved with a potato ricer – like a giant garlic press (see page 50). Pressing through the fine blade of a meat mincer also gives a good result, as does pushing through a sieve. When mashed, beat well with a wooden spoon or a strong wire whisk.

Do not, under any circumstances, use a food processor, or you will end up with something that looks like wallpaper paste! For a lighter texture, heat liquids such as milk or cream before beating in.

If using the mash to make piped potato toppings and garnishes, add beaten egg yolk to produce a glazed, golden colour.

Classic Mashed Potato Recipe

Scrub 1 kg medium-sized floury potatoes, then boil in lightly salted water for 20 to 30 minutes until tender. Drain, cool and peel, then mash with 125 g butter. Reheat, season, then beat in 300 ml hot milk.

New Potato Crush Recipe

Boil 500 g small waxy or new potatoes until tender, then crush lightly with a fork, season, then stir in butter or olive oil.

Flavoured Mashes

The basic, delicious mashed potato can be flavoured with any number of herbs, spices, vegetables and other ingredients.

Olive Oil Mash

Mash boiled potatoes with warmed olive oil, salt, pepper and (optional) hot cream and grated Parmesan cheese – delicious and healthier than potato mashed with butter.

Saffron Mash

For a fragrant, bright yellow mash, add a few strands of saffron to the water when boiling peeled potatoes, or infuse the saffron in milk or cream before mixing.

Pesto Mash

Add 2 tablespoons pesto to plain mash.

Herb Oil Mash

For strong flavour and bright colour, purée parsley (shown left), basil, chives, mint, coriander or other soft herbs with olive oil in a food processor, then add to the mash.

Garlic Mash

Roast garlic cloves, squeeze the flesh out of the skins, crush them well, then stir them through the mashed potato.

Cheese Mash

Stir through grated Parmesan or a melting cheese such as fontina or Gruyère, or a crumbled blue cheese such as Gorgonzola or Dolcelatte.

Mustard Mash

Add 2 tablespoons wholegrain mustard to basic mashed potato.

Other Mashes

Stir through puréed parsnips, celeriac, sweet potato, swede, turnip, beetroot, salsify, pumpkin, artichokes (globe and Jerusalem), cabbage and other greens, fennel, celery, mushrooms (wild or cultivated – porcini are especially good), aubergine, leeks or roasted onions. Try spices and flavourings such as nutmeg, horseradish, truffles, olive tapenade, sun-dried tomatoes, chillies, sweet peppers, nuts (raw or roasted, then ground), lemon, orange, chopped or puréed apple, sweetcorn, rocket, watercress, mashed anchovy or a cream of dried salt cod.

oven-cooked
potatoes

**From roasting
to baking –
from gratins
to pies**

Roasting Potatoes

The perfect roast potato has a crisp crunchy surface and a soft, fluffy interior. Floury varieties are best for roasting, though small waxy ones are also used in some cuisines, notably modern Italian. Roast potatoes with onions (either whole or cut into wedges), garlic cloves in their skins, thyme or rosemary for extra flavour. If roasted with meat, the result will be less crisp, but will have excellent flavour.

Preparation
Potatoes can be roasted with or without the skins, but if peeled and cut into chunks, the pieces should be uniform, so they cook at the same rate. Par-boiling first gives a soft interior and crisp edge. After par-boiling, return them to the pan and swirl them to roughen the edges or, holding them in a clean cloth, score them with a fork.

Oils and Fats
The oil or fat used to cook potatoes is a matter of personal taste and regional tradition. Olive, vegetable, sunflower or peanut oils are now the most common choice, largely for health reasons. However duck and goose fat famously give the most wonderful flavour. Lard and dripping, now rarely used, also give very good flavour.

Roasting Method, Times and Temperatures
Put oil or fat in a roasting tin large enough to hold the potatoes in a single layer. Heat on top of the stove or in the oven. Add the potatoes to the hot oil (take care in case it sputters). Season, then turn to coat with oil. Cook in a preheated oven at 220°C (425°F) Gas Mark 7 for 1 hour, turning occasionally, until crisp outside and tender inside. The time depends on the size of the potatoes.

Baking Potatoes

Potatoes baked whole have a fluffy interior with a crispy skin. Serve smaller ones with grilled or roasted meats. Larger ones are served on their own, slit lengthways, and filled with flavourings ranging from simple cold butter to cheese, beans or canned tuna. Floury varieties are best.

Preparation
Scrub the potatoes, then prick with a fork. A metal skewer can also be pushed into each potato. For a crunchy crust, roll the potatoes gently in sea salt before baking.

Baking Method, Times and Temperatures
Put the potato directly on the oven shelf or wrap in foil. Cook in a preheated oven at 200°C (400°F) Gas Mark 6 for 1–1¼ hours or until soft in the centre when tested (or, if using a skewer, it can be easily removed). To cook a large number at once, increase to 220°C (425°F) Gas Mark 7.

Microwaving
Baking in a microwave will not give the crisp skin that results from oven-baking, but is a very quick method if you're in a hurry. Prick the potato all over with a fork, put on a piece of kitchen paper, and microwave on high for 8–10 minutes (15 minutes for 2 potatoes, about 20 to 25 minutes for 4 potatoes), or until the potato is tender when tested. Let stand 2–3 minutes before using. Baking times vary according to the oven wattage and the size, shape and variety of the potatoes.

Potatoes Baked in the Coals
This potato baking method is popular in Australia. As part of a beach or garden barbecue, whole potatoes are placed in the coals of a (wood-fired) barbecue. To serve, the black, ash-covered skins are broken open, then sea salt and a spoonful of butter or olive oil is added.

Potato Wedges and Potato Skins

Cut the potatoes into wedges, brush with olive oil, season and cook at 200°C (400°F) Gas Mark 6 for 20–25 minutes, turning once or twice. Serve as a vegetable or dip. To make potato skins, bake in the usual way, then cut into wedges lengthways. Scoop out the flesh (use for another purpose) leaving some attached to the skin. Brush the skins with oil and roast or deep-fry until crisp and golden. Drain on kitchen paper and serve warm with a dip.

Gratins and Pies

To make a gratin, potatoes are layered in a dish with cream, milk or butter, topped with cheese and/or breadcrumbs, and baked until the top is crisp and golden and the centre creamy. Other vegetables, especially root vegetables, can be layered alternately with the potato.
Dishes such as Fish Pies, Shepherd's Pies and Cottage Pies are fish, lamb or beef stews respectively, topped with mashed potato, then baked until lightly golden. A vegetarian version can be made with a vegetable ragout, topped with a layer of mashed potato, then baked.

Shallow-fried Potatoes

Sauté Potatoes

A great French potato dish. Raw potato is sautéed gently in fats such as butter, oil, a mixture of the two, duck or goose fat, clarified butter, lard or bacon fat mixed with oil, then served sprinkled with flakes of sea salt.

Deep-fried Potatoes

Floury potato varieties are best.

Use a deep-fryer or large, deep pan, and never use oil at a depth of more than a third to a half full. A wok, one-third full of oil, is also good – you can move the potatoes around so they cook evenly. Always reheat oil to the required temperature between batches, and lower the potatoes gently into the oil to prevent splashing. A frying basket, wire scoop, or slotted spoon allows the potatoes to be turned and lifted easily. Do not overcrowd the pan, or the heat will be reduced and the potatoes boil rather than fry, absorb too much oil, and become greasy and soggy. Fry at 180–190°C. If fried at too low a heat, the potatoes will absorb too much oil: if too high, they will burn.

Oils and Fats

Peanut or corn oil cook at a high heat without burning. Olive oil is wonderful but extravagant. Sunflower oil, safflower oil and lard are also used. Always use clean oil, strain after use, and when re-using, remember what was cooked in it previously (to avoid fishy tastes!)

Safety First!

Always dry the potato well, as excess water makes the oil sputter and boil. Never leave the pan unattended and clean up any spills immediately. Turn the handle away from the edge of the stove so it can't be bumped. If the oil starts to smoke, turn off the heat immediately. In the event of a fire, turn off the heat and cover the pan with a lid, baking sheet, or a thick, damp cloth. Do not move the pan or use water to extinguish the fire. Let the pan cool completely before moving it.

Deep-fried Chips

Perfect chips are twice-cooked. Cut potatoes into long strips 5 mm–1.5 cm thick, rinse well in cold water to remove the starch, then dry well. Fry in hot oil at 160°C for 5 minutes until tender but pale, then drain well. Raise the heat to 190°C and cook again for 1–2 minutes until crisp and golden. Check temperatures with a deep-frying thermometer or test-fry a cube of bread: it will turn golden in 1 minute at 180°C or in 40 seconds at 190°C.

Potato Crisps

Very finely sliced potatoes, rinsed of starch, then patted dry, are deep-fried until crisp and golden. These are best cut on a mandolin (see page 137) – useful and efficient for finely slicing vegetables. It has a wooden, metal or plastic frame with a set of adjustable cutting blades; smooth for slicing and cutting chips, or fluted for cutting gaufrettes and straw potatoes. The best have a protective guard between you and the vegetables, so you don't cut yourself. Mandolins can be expensive, but cheaper plastic Chinese and Japanese brands are sold in oriental shops (even top chefs use them!)

Pommes Soufflés

Slice thin rounds of potato on a mandolin, then twice-fry as for chips, so they puff up like a soufflé.

Gaufrettes or Waffle Potatoes

Using a mandolin, slice the potato once on the fluted cutting blade, then turn the potato 90° and slice again to produce a finely latticed slice. Deep-fry until crisp and golden.

Straw Potatoes (Matchsticks)

Shred very finely, then deep-fry.

Potato Ribbons

A variation on straw potatoes (see page 43 for the cooking method).

Potato Baskets

Potato baskets are made by lining a wire basket with unrinsed, very thinly sliced potatoes, then pressing a smaller wire basket inside. The whole thing is deep-fried until crisp. Special utensils are available, but a simple substitute can be made with large and small sieves that fit snugly together.

Croquettes and Fritters

Balls, rounds, or ovals of mashed potatoes can be coated with flour, egg and breadcrumbs, polenta, chopped nuts or crushed vermicelli, then deep-fried until crisp and golden.

fried and deep-fried
potatoes

From chips to rösti – from crisps to croquettes

the
americas

South America was the original homeland of the potato. It was taken to Europe by Spanish and English adventurers, then by the Portuguese to West Africa and Asia. Pre-Columbian cultures cultivated **hundreds of varieties**, and even more are still growing wild.

These little stacks of tostadas are usually made with corn tortillas, but they are wonderful made with potato wafers as a modern alternative.

tostadas

crispy potato tostadas
with salmon and scallop seviche

8 small scallops, or 4 larger ones sliced crossways (roes removed)

500 g salmon fillet, carefully deboned with tweezers

300 ml freshly squeezed lime juice

150 ml freshly squeezed orange juice

150 ml freshly squeezed lemon juice

1 red chilli, deseeded and very finely chopped

1 small red onion, very thinly sliced

½ avocado, peeled and chopped

2 tomatoes, skinned and chopped

2 tablespoons chopped fresh coriander, plus sprigs, to serve

2 tablespoons extra-virgin olive oil

salt and freshly ground black pepper

Potato Wafers:

500 g potatoes

50 g butter, melted, plus extra, for greasing

salt and freshly ground black pepper

Serves 4

Cut away the small sac attached to the scallop. Slice the salmon as thinly as possible. Place all the fish slices in a shallow non-metallic container. Mix the lime, orange and lemon juices together and pour over. Cover and chill for 4–6 hours. To make the potato wafers, grate the potato finely, but do not wash. Drain in a sieve, then place the potato in a clean kitchen towel and squeeze well to extract the moisture. Put the potato in a bowl, stir in the butter and season with salt and pepper. Mix well, then divide the mixture into 12.

Lightly grease a baking sheet with butter. Put an 11 cm plain pastry cutter on the sheet and spoon in one portion of the grated potato mixture inside the ring. Spread evenly with the back of a teaspoon. Lift the ring and repeat with the remaining mixture to make 12 wafers. (You may need 2 sheets.)

Place the sheet in a preheated oven 200 °C (400°F) Gas Mark 6 and cook for 5–6 minutes. Remove from the oven and turn the wafers over with a palette knife. Return to the oven and continue cooking for a further 3–4 minutes or until both sides are golden brown and crispy.

Make sure the fish is completely opaque. Thirty minutes to 1 hour before serving, drain off the liquid and carefully stir in the chilli, onion, avocado, tomato, chopped coriander and olive oil. Season and set aside.

To make one serving, put a potato wafer on a small plate. Top with a little of the fish mixture, top with another potato wafer, followed by more fish mixture and a final potato wafer, until you have a 5-layered tower. Repeat to make 4 servings altogether, sprinkle with sprigs of coriander, then serve.

Though creamy mayonnaise-style sauces are the traditional dressings for cold potato salads, modern American chefs have been successfully experimenting with highly flavoured dressings based on extra-virgin olive oil, now known to be the healthiest form of oil. Potatoes have a special affinity with strong flavours.

roasted warm potato salad

1 kg small new or salad potatoes

125 ml extra-virgin olive oil

1 small red onion, finely chopped

25 g pitted black olives, finely chopped

1½ tablespoons capers, rinsed and drained

6 sun-dried tomatoes in oil, drained and chopped

5 tablespoons chopped fresh flat-leaf parsley

1 tablespoon balsamic vinegar

sea salt flakes and freshly ground black pepper

Serves 4–6

Variation:

Blue Potato Salad

1 kg blue, purple or black potatoes

125 g butter

salt and freshly ground black pepper

chopped herbs (optional), to serve

Place the potatoes in a roasting tin, add 2 tablespoons of the olive oil, sprinkle with sea salt and toss well to coat.

Cook in a preheated oven at 200°C (400°F) Gas Mark 6 for 25–30 minutes, or until tender, turning the potatoes occasionally.

While the potatoes are cooking, put all the remaining ingredients in a large bowl, mix well and season with salt and pepper.

Remove the potatoes from the oven, crush each potato slightly with a fork and cut in half. Toss the still-warm potatoes in the bowl of dressing, mix well and serve either warm or cold.

Variation:

Blue Potato Salad

Boil or roast the potatoes in their skins until tender – the time will depend on the variety, age and size of the potatoes.

Serve tossed in butter and chopped fresh herbs (optional). Purple or black potatoes are best served in the same way, so their extraordinary colour can be best appreciated.

gingered seafood chowder
with red roe cream and poppyseed crackers

Potatoes are native to South America, so it is hardly surprising that some of the most exciting potato recipes come from the Americas. Chowders are typical New England soups – the New World versions of fishermen's stews such as *bouillabaisse* and *bourride*. Vital ingredients include potatoes and bacon, and usually seafood of some kind, though chowders can also be made with chicken, or for vegetarians. Clam chowders are traditional, but prawns and scallops can also be used to make equally delicious chowders.

25 g butter
50 g streaky bacon, cut into small strips
1 onion, chopped
1 small garlic clove, crushed
2.5 cm fresh root ginger, peeled and finely grated
1 tablespoon plain flour
1 litre milk
500 g potatoes, cut into 1.5 cm cubes
1 bay leaf
250 g fresh scallops with roes, whites cleaned and sliced into 2–3 pieces crossways if large (reserve the roes)
600 ml single cream
12 uncooked king prawns, shelled and deveined
chopped chives and parsley, to serve

Poppyseed Crackers:
250 g plain flour
1 pinch chilli powder
1 teaspoon sugar
1 teaspoon salt
25 g butter, cut into small pieces
1 tablespoon poppyseeds, finely ground in a spice or coffee grinder
150 ml milk
sea salt flakes
Serves 4

1 To make the poppyseed crackers, sieve the flour, chilli powder, sugar and salt into a large bowl. Rub in the butter until it resembles fine breadcrumbs. Stir in the poppyseeds. Slowly add the milk to form a soft but firm dough.

2 Divide the dough in half and roll out to 2 large rectangles, 40 x 30 cm each. Trim the edges, then transfer to a lightly greased baking sheet or sheets. Score the surface into 5 cm squares and sprinkle with a few sea salt flakes.

3 Bake in a preheated oven at 200°C (400°F) Gas Mark 6 for 6–8 minutes until golden. Turn the pieces over with a palette knife and cook for 5–6 minutes more. Transfer to a wire rack, let cool, then break the crackers apart.

4 To make the chowder, melt the butter in a large pan, add the bacon and cook until crispy. Add the onion, garlic and ginger and sauté gently for 5–10 minutes until softened and translucent but not coloured.

5 Add the flour. Cook, stirring, for 1–2 minutes without colouring. Stir in a little milk until smooth, then add the remainder. Add potatoes and bay leaf, simmer 8–10 minutes until tender, remove from the heat and season to taste.

6 Put 4 tablespoons of the cooking liquid into a small pan, bring to a simmer, add the red roes and cook for 30 seconds or until just firm. Remove from the heat and purée the roes and liquid in a small blender until smooth.

7 Reserve about 4 tablespoons of the scallop mixture and set aside. Pour the remainder into the chowder, add the cream, and bring slowly back to the boil. Add the prawns and cook for 1 minute – no longer or they will overcook.

8 Add the scallops and cook for a further minute. Serve the chowder in individual bowls sprinkled with the herbs, drizzled with the reserved red roe purée and accompanied by the poppyseed crackers.

GINGERED SEAFOOD CHOWDER **21**

potatoes en papillote
scented with fresh herbs

This traditional French cooking method has been enthusiastically adopted by modern American chefs. Cooking in a parcel means that all the flavour and goodness of the potatoes is retained as they cook in their own steam. They should be opened at the table by the guests to relish the wonderful aromas rising from the scented packages. New potatoes are best used as quickly as possible after buying, which is why good supermarkets have a very short sell-by date, often only 2–3 days after they go on display.

Cut out 4 sheets of greaseproof or parchment paper, 30 x 38 cm each, and fold in half. Draw a large curve to make a heart shape when unfolded. Cut around the line and open out.

Place a quarter of the potatoes on one half of each piece of paper. Dot the butter evenly all over, sprinkle with sea salt and add a herb sprig to each one.

Brush the edges of the paper lightly with the beaten egg and fold over. Starting from the rounded end, pleat the edges together so that each parcel is completely sealed. Twist the ends together. Put the parcels on a baking sheet and cook in a preheated oven at 200°C (400°F) Gas Mark 6 for 25–30 minutes until the parcels are well puffed and the potatoes are tender. Serve immediately.

500 g very small new potatoes

50 g unsalted butter

4 sprigs fresh herbs such as thyme, tarragon, chervil, mint or rosemary

1 egg, beaten

sea salt

Serves 4

empanaditas

Empanadas are pastry turnovers popular in Spanish and Latin American cooking. They usually have savoury fillings, but can sometimes have a fruit filling and be served as a pudding. Usually baked or deep-fried, they can be very large indeed, or very tiny – when they are known as *empanaditas*, and are particularly good to eat with drinks. Serve them on their own, or with a spicy fruit salsa, such as papaya, mango, peach or pineapple mixed with red onion and chilli. Salsas are the spicy, fashionable Mexican contribution to the world's culinary repertoire.

250 g plain flour
½ teaspoon salt
100 g butter, melted
2–2½ tablespoons water
vegetable oil, for deep-frying
Spicy Potato Filling:
2 medium potatoes, cut in 5 mm dice
3 spring onions, chopped
125 g canned sweetcorn kernels, drained
1–2 green chillies, deseeded and finely chopped (optional)
75 g ricotta or goats' cheese, crumbled
1 tablespoon chopped fresh marjoram
½ teaspoon paprika
salt and freshly ground black pepper
Makes 16

empanaditas

1 Parboil the potatoes in a saucepan of lightly salted boiling water for about 2–3 minutes, drain well and let cool. Mix the remaining filling ingredients in a bowl, stir in the cooled potatoes, season with salt and pepper and set aside.

2 Sieve the flour and salt into a large bowl, stir in the butter and add enough water to form a soft but firm dough. Knead briefly, wrap in clingfilm and leave to rest for 30 minutes at room temperature.

3 On a lightly floured surface, roll out the dough to about 2.5 mm thick, then cut out 16 rounds, 12 cm in diameter, using a small saucer. Knead and re-roll any trimmings. Put 1 tablespoon filling on each round, a little off-centre.

4 Dampen the edges of the pastry with a little water and fold in half over the filling. Using the prongs of a fork, press the edges together to seal them. Place the *empanaditas* on a tray and refrigerate for about 30 minutes to 1 hour.

5 Heat the oil in a deep pan to 190°C (375°F) or until a cube of bread browns in 40 seconds. Fry the empanaditas in batches, turning once, for 3–5 minutes, or until golden brown. Drain on kitchen paper and serve.

The baked potato, roasted whole in its skin, then split and topped with a variety of delicious fillings, is a great American staple that's been enthusiastically adopted in other parts of the world. In this version, the flesh is scooped out of the shells, mixed with whisked egg and other ingredients, then spooned back into the shell and baked again. The result is a sublime fluffy filling.

baked potatoes
with fluffy soufflé fillings

4 large baking potatoes

sea salt flakes

15 g butter, diced

75 ml milk

2 eggs, separated

salt and freshly ground black pepper

Smoked Salmon Filling (shown left):

100 g smoked salmon, cut into strips

2 tablespoons chopped fresh chives

1 tablespoon capers, rinsed, drained
and coarsely chopped

4 sun-dried tomatoes in oil,
drained and finely chopped

Anchovy Gruyère Filling (variation):

8 anchovy fillets, mashed with a fork

125 g Gruyère cheese, cut in 1 cm cubes

2 tablespoons chopped
fresh flat-leaf parsley

25 g black olives,
pitted and finely chopped

Serves 4

Wash the potatoes thoroughly, shaking off most of the water. Prick them all over with a fork and sprinkle with sea salt flakes. (This is optional but gives a wonderful crispy crust) Cook in a preheated oven at 200°C (400°F) Gas Mark 6 for about 1 hour or until cooked through.

Reduce the oven temperature to 180°C (350°F) Gas Mark 4.

Mix the filling ingredients together and reserve.

Whilst the potatoes are still hot, cut off a 1 cm slice and discard, or reserve for another purpose.

Using a spoon, scoop out the flesh leaving a 5 mm shell. Push the scooped-out flesh through a potato ricer, mouli or sieve into a large bowl. Place the shells on a baking sheet.

Add the butter to the potato flesh and mix well. Bring the milk to just below boiling point, then beat into the potato mixture. Beat the egg yolks and add to the potato, mixing well.

Stir in the filling mixture and season to taste with salt and pepper. Whisk the egg whites until stiff but not dry. Fold in a third of the beaten egg whites to loosen the mixture, then gently fold in the rest.

Spoon the mixture back into the shells, heaping the tops. Put in the oven and cook for 15–20 minutes until slightly risen and lightly browned on top.

I found this delicious tart in New Mexico. The chilli kick is quite subtle – roasting the chillies softens the flavour. Potatoes are great partners for the ~~ve~~ of chilli, and you can also add chilli to the pastry for added zest.

chilli potato tart
with roasted tomatoes and garlic

750 g ripe red plum tomatoes, halved lengthways, then deseeded

3 tablespoons extra-virgin olive oil

4 whole garlic cloves, unpeeled

1 large red chilli

1½ teaspoons sea salt flakes

1 tablespoons caster sugar

500 g waxy potatoes, boiled in their skins for 15 minutes, then peeled and sliced thinly

300 ml crème fraîche, lightly whipped and seasoned with salt and pepper

salt and freshly ground black pepper

Chilli Pastry:

200 g plain flour

a pinch of salt

100 g unsalted butter

25 g finely grated Parmesan cheese

1 red chilli, deseeded and very finely chopped (optional)

Serves 6

To roast the tomatoes, lightly brush a baking sheet with some of the olive oil and add the tomatoes, cut side up. Add the garlic and whole chilli and sprinkle with the remaining olive oil.

Sprinkle the salt and sugar evenly over the tomatoes and cook in a preheated oven at 180°C (350°F) Gas Mark 4. Remove the garlic after 10–15 minutes when soft and squeeze the flesh into a bowl. Remove the chilli after 15–20 minutes when the skin is blistered and slightly charred. Leave the tomatoes for 45–50 minutes until very soft and slightly charred. Cool the chillies a little, then peel, deseed, chop finely and add to the garlic. Scoop the tomato flesh out of the skins into the bowl, mash with a fork and add seasoning.

To make the pastry, sieve the flour and salt into a bowl. Rub in the butter until it resembles fine crumbs. Stir in the Parmesan and chilli, if using. Add enough cold water to make a firm dough, then roll out on a lightly floured surface and use to line a greased, 25 cm fluted tart tin. Lightly prick the base with a fork. Chill for 30 minutes, then line with foil and baking beans. Heat a baking sheet on the middle shelf of a preheated oven at 200°C (400°F) Gas Mark 6. Put the tart shell on the sheet, bake for 10–15 minutes then remove the foil and beans.

Spread the tomato mixture evenly on the tart base, then cover with the potato slices in concentric circles. Increase the heat to 230°C (450°F) Gas Mark 8. Pour the crème fraîche over the potato and bake for 8–10 minutes until the top is lightly golden.

These little fried cakes of potato and chorizo with a crisp corn salsa are based on a dish I found in Mexico. *Queso fresco* is a mild fresh cheese often used in Mexican cooking. I have substituted fresh goats' cheese, which has an affinity with spicy food though it isn't traditional. You could also use a feta cheese, as long as it's not too salty.

tortitas

tortitas de papa
with chorizo and corn salsa verde

750 g potatoes, unpeeled, scrubbed well
3 chorizo sausages, peeled and crumbled
1 garlic clove, crushed
4 spring onions, chopped
250 g goats' cheese, crumbled
1 egg, beaten
75 g fine dry breadcrumbs
olive oil, for cooking
salt and freshly ground black pepper

Corn Salsa Verde:
1 tablespoon Dijon mustard
1 tablespoon lime juice or wine vinegar
150 ml extra-virgin olive oil
2 tablespoons capers, rinsed and chopped
75 g canned sweetcorn kernels, drained
2 spring onions, finely chopped
1–2 garlic cloves, chopped very finely
6 tablespoons chopped
fresh flat-leaf parsley
6 tablespoons chopped fresh coriander
1–2 green chillies, finely chopped
sea salt and freshly ground black pepper

Serves 6

Place the potatoes in a large saucepan, bring to the boil, then simmer for 15–20 minutes or until tender. Drain well and when cool enough to handle, peel and pass through a potato ricer, mouli or a sieve into a large bowl.

Heat a non-stick frying pan, add the chorizo and sauté gently for 5–10 minutes until the fat renders. Lift out the chorizo with a slotted spoon, let it cool slightly, then add to the bowl of potato. Add the garlic, spring onions and goats' cheese and mix. Add the egg, salt and pepper and mix well.

Divide the mixture into 18 parts and form into small flat cakes. Roll each potato cake in the breadcrumbs, pressing gently so the crumbs stick. Set aside while you make the salsa.

To make the salsa verde, put the mustard in a small bowl and whisk in the lime juice or wine vinegar. Continue whisking, adding the olive oil in a thin stream until amalgamated. Stir in the remaining ingredients, then add salt and pepper to taste.

Heat the oil in a large frying pan and fry the potato cakes in batches until golden brown all over (about 8–10 minutes). Drain on kitchen paper and keep warm while you cook the remaining potato cakes.

Serve with the salsa and a crisp salad, such as the mizuna, rocket and baby spinach leaves shown here.

This American classic is named after the deep dish in which it is cooked. An American chef taught me this version with fluffy potato pastry.

chicken pot pie
with porcini mushrooms and potato pastry

2 sprigs of tarragon

I free-range chicken, 1.5–2 kg

3 carrots, chopped

2 celery sticks, chopped

I bay leaf

a few parsley stalks

I onion, chopped

Porcini Filling:

15 g dried porcini mushrooms

15 g butter

2 onions, chopped

4 slices pancetta or streaky bacon, cut into small strips

15 g plain flour

2 tablespoons lemon juice

150 ml double cream

2 tablespoons chopped fresh tarragon

salt and freshly ground black pepper

Potato Pastry:

175 g plain flour

a pinch of salt

75 g butter, diced

175 g mashed potato

I egg yolk, beaten

Serves 4

Stuff the tarragon in the chicken and put in a large pan with the carrots, celery, bay leaf, parsley stalks and onion. Cover with 2–3 litres water, bring to the boil, then simmer gently for I hour until the vegetables are tender.

Transfer the chicken to a plate and cool slightly. Strip the meat from the chicken and separate into evenly sized pieces. Divide the meat between 4 small pie dishes. Strain the stock into a clean pan, discarding the vegetables and herbs. Bring to the boil and simmer until reduced by half.

Put the porcini in a bowl, pour over about 250 ml boiling water, soak for 20 minutes, then strain, reserving the liquid. Chop the porcini finely. Strain the reserved liquid through coffee filter paper set over a measuring jug. Make up to 600 ml with stock, reserving the remaining stock for another use.

Melt the butter in a pan, add the onions and porcini and cook gently for about 3 minutes. Add the pancetta or bacon and cook for 2–3 minutes to soften the onion and lightly colour the bacon. Add the flour and cook without browning for 1–2 minutes. Gradually add the stock, stirring until thick and smooth. Add the lemon juice, cream and tarragon, bring to the boil, season to taste, then remove from the heat. Let cool slightly, then divide between the pie dishes.

To make the pastry, sieve the flour and salt into a bowl, then rub in the butter until it resembles fine crumbs. Mix in the potato to form a soft but firm dough. Roll out to 5 mm thick then cut 4 rounds slightly larger than the pie dishes. Brush the edges of the dishes with water then cover with a pastry lid. Trim the edges, roll out any excess pastry and use to decorate. Make a small steam hole in the centre of each pie and brush the tops with beaten egg yolk. Cook in a preheated oven at 200°C (400°F) Gas Mark 6 for 15 minutes, reduce to 180°C (350°F) Gas Mark 4 and cook for a further 15–20 minutes or until the pastry is crisp and golden brown.

Cajun cooking, from America's South, is a combination of French and Southern cuisines – full of wonderful, complex, spicy flavours. Commercial Cajun spice mixes are widely available, but I prefer the home-made quality of the flavourings in this recipe, with fresh onion and garlic, as well as the spices and herbs added separately.

cajun potato wedges
with spicy lemon and onions

4 potatoes, unpeeled, cut into 4 or 6 wedges
1 lemon, cut into 6 wedges
8 whole garlic cloves, unpeeled
2 red onions, cut lengthways through the root end into small wedges
4–5 bay leaves
3 tablespoons freshly squeezed lemon juice
4 tablespoons water
1 tablespoon tomato purée
½ teaspoon freshly ground black pepper
1 teaspoon salt
1 teaspoon paprika
½ teaspoon cayenne pepper
1 teaspoon dried oregano
1 teaspoon dried or fresh thyme leaves
½ teaspoon ground cumin
4 tablespoons olive oil
Serves 4

Bring a large pan of lightly salted water to the boil. Add the potato wedges, bring back to the boil and cook for 3 minutes. Drain well and place in a large roasting tin with the lemon wedges, garlic, onions and bay leaves.

Put the lemon juice, water and tomato purée into a small bowl. Add the spices and herbs and mix together well. Pour the spice mixture over the potatoes in the tin and toss together to coat. Drizzle over the oil and cook in a preheated oven at 200°C (400°F) Gas Mark 6 for 35–40 minutes, or until the potatoes are tender and all the liquid has been absorbed. Turn the mixture frequently with a metal spatula or fish slice.

Serve hot with grilled meats.

One of the world's best-known potato dishes, in which cooked potatoes – mashed, grated or cubed – are fried slowly in oil, bacon fat or butter. Use a heat-diffusing mat to ensure slow, even cooking. The artichokes are not traditional, but are utterly delicious!

hash browns

3 lemons (2 squeezed, 1 halved)
12 baby artichokes*
6 tablespoons olive oil or clarified butter (or a mixture of both)
4 garlic cloves, finely sliced
1 tablespoon fresh thyme leaves
500 g floury potatoes, boiled in their skins, then peeled and cut into 1 cm dice
salt and freshly ground black pepper
Serves 4

Variation:
Classic Hash Browns
1 small onion, finely chopped
6 tablespoons clarified butter or olive oil
750 g cooked floury potatoes, peeled and cut into 1 cm dice
salt and freshly ground black pepper

*If using sliced artichokes bottled in oil, cook the garlic briefly until softened, then add the artichokes, thyme and potatoes and continue as in the main recipe.

Pour the lemon juice into a bowl large enough to hold all the artichokes and half-fill the bowl with cold water.

Cut off the artichoke stems 2.5 cm from the base of the globes. Slice off the the top of the pointed leaves. Remove 2–3 layers of outer leaves to expose the tender yellow leaves, then rub the cut surfaces with the lemon and put the artichokes in the bowl of acidulated water. If the artichokes are large, scoop out the hairy centre chokes with a teaspoon and discard. One by one, remove the artichokes from the water, cut finely lengthways into 2.5 mm slices, then replace in the water. When ready to cook, drain well. Heat the oil or butter in a large heavy-based frying pan. Add the garlic, thyme and artichokes, cover and cook gently, stirring occasionally, for 6–8 minutes or until just tender.

Add the potatoes, spreading evenly over the pan. Season, then cook over low heat for 15–20 minutes. Press down frequently with a spatula, shake the pan occasionally, and cook until the base is crisp and golden.

Cover the pan with a large plate or tray, flip over, then slide the hash browns back into the pan. Cook the other side, pressing down, until golden and crisp. Serve with grilled fish or meat.

Variation:
Classic Hash Browns
Sauté the onion in the butter or oil until softened, then add the potatoes and seasoning and proceed as in the main recipe.

europe

Elizabethan heroes **Drake** and **Raleigh** have been credited with introducing the **potato** to Europe from South America, while Irish immigrants took it back to North America in the 1700s. **Parmentier** made it fashionable in France, where some potato dishes are now called *Parmentier* in his honour.

fish and chips
tuna strips with potato ribbons

There can be no more British dish than fish and chips – and it's also popular in former British colonies around the world. The batter should be light, the chips should be thick-cut and twice-fried to delicious crispness (see page 12). Ideally, they should be sprinkled with salt and vinegar, wrapped in newspaper and eaten sitting on the sea wall in a fishing village in Scotland. This recipe is a modern update of the great classic. Though tuna, the king of fishes, isn't caught in British waters, it makes a great alternative to the usual cod or haddock. These crispy, deep-fried, curled potato ribbons are a delicious variation on traditional chips, and don't need to be twice-fried.

1 kg floury potatoes, peeled

500 g piece of fresh tuna

sea salt

vegetable oil, for deep-frying

Sesame Batter:

50 g sesame seeds

2 large egg yolks

500 ml ice water

250 g plain flour, plus extra
for dusting

Lemon and Sesame Mayonnaise:

1 egg yolk

1 tablespoon fresh lemon juice

½ teaspoon Dijon mustard

150 ml vegetable oil

1 teaspoon sesame oil (optional)

finely grated zest of 1 small lemon

salt and freshly ground black pepper

Serves 6–8

To make the batter, first put the sesame seeds in a dry frying pan over a low heat and cook, tossing continuously until they are golden brown (take care they don't burn). Transfer to a large plate to cool.

To make the mayonnaise, put the egg yolk, lemon juice and mustard in a food processor and pulse until blended. Mix the vegetable and sesame oils and, with the motor running, add the oil in a slow, thin stream. When the mayonnaise is thick, scrape into a bowl and stir in the lemon zest, salt and pepper.

To make the potato ribbons, cut each potato into 1 cm slices. Using a potato peeler, peel around the edges of each slice to form long strips. Cut off lengths of the strips, tie into knots or bows, then put in a large bowl of cold water. Alternatively, cut around the potato as you would an apple to form long strips. Cut the tuna into 1 cm slices and cut the slices into thin strips, 1 cm wide.

Rinse and drain the potato ribbons 2–3 times, then dry well on clean tea towels. Heat the oil in a pan or deep-fryer to 190°C (375°F) or until a cube of bread browns in 40 seconds. Deep-fry the potato ribbons in batches for 3–4 minutes until crisp and golden. Drain well on kitchen paper, sprinkle with sea salt and keep them warm.

To complete the batter, put the egg yolks in a large bowl, add a little of the ice water, mix well, then whisk in the remaining water. Add the flour and sesame seeds and stir with a fork until just mixed. Don't worry if it is slightly lumpy – it is better under-mixed than over-mixed.

Reheat the oil to 190°C (375°F). Place a little flour on a plate or tray, then dip each strip of tuna into the flour, shaking off any excess. Dip into the batter, then deep-fry the strips, a few at a time, turning occasionally, for 2–3 minutes until the flesh is tender and the batter is crispy and lightly golden. Drain on kitchen paper and serve immediately with the potato ribbons and the sesame mayonnaise.

Antoine Parmentier, a military pharmacist, popularized the potato in France in the early 1700s. The French were suspicious of this new American vegetable, so Parmentier posted guards around his fields during the day, leaving it unprotected at night. Needless to say, the potatoes were stolen and soon became both popular and fashionable.

potage parmentier
with parsley oil and croûtons

50 g unsalted butter

500 g floury potatoes, peeled and very thinly sliced

1 onion, thinly sliced

1 bay leaf

900 ml milk

salt and freshly ground black pepper

Parsley Oil:

75 g fresh flat-leaf parsley, washed and dried

125 ml extra-virgin olive oil

Bacon-flavoured Croûtons:

3 tablespoons olive oil or 25 g unsalted butter

4 slices pancetta or rindless streaky bacon

2 slices of bread, crusts removed, cut or broken into 1 cm pieces

Serves 4

To make the parsley oil, bring a pan of water to the boil, add the parsley and blanch for 5–10 seconds. Drain and refresh in plenty of cold water. Drain well, then squeeze dry in a clean tea towel. Chop the parsley and put in a blender. Add the olive oil and purée until very smooth. Either leave as is, or strain first through a fine sieve, then again through 2 layers of muslin or a paper coffee filter. Pour into a clean bottle and use within 1 week.

To make the soup (*potage*), melt the butter in a large, heavy-based saucepan, add the potatoes and onion, stir, cover and cook without colouring for 5–8 minutes, stirring occasionally, until the onion is softened and translucent.

Add the bay leaf, milk, salt and pepper, bring to the boil, reduce the heat, cover and simmer for 15–20 minutes. Remove from the heat, discard the bay leaf, pour into a blender and purée until smooth. Strain through a very fine sieve into a clean pan.

To make the croûtons, heat the oil or melt the butter in a large frying pan over a moderate heat. Add the pancetta or bacon and sauté for 5–6 minutes until crisp. Remove with a slotted spoon and drain on kitchen paper. Add the bread to the pan and cook, turning frequently, until crisp and golden. Drain on kitchen paper. Reheat the soup, season and serve, drizzled with parsley oil. Drop the croûtons and pancetta into the soup or serve separately.

Pillow-soft potato pancakes make the perfect accompaniment for gravad lax, a favourite Scandinavian dish. The word means 'buried salmon' in Swedish, but other fish can also be used, such as trout, herring and the mackerel used here. The potato pancakes are also a wonderful breakfast or brunch dish, served with bacon, eggs, or as an accompaniment to meat or fish.

gravad lax

potato pancakes
with mackerel gravad lax

500 g floury potatoes
3 beaten eggs, plus 2 beaten egg whites
50 g self-raising flour
125 ml hot milk (just below boiling)
freshly grated nutmeg
sea salt and freshly ground black pepper
corn oil or clarified butter, for frying

Mackerel Gravad Lax:

2 tablespoons coarse sea salt
2 tablespoons light soft brown sugar
2 teaspoons white peppercorns, crushed
1 bunch fresh dill, chopped
6 large mackerel fillets, about 250 g
each, bones removed with tweezers

Dill Cream:

200 g crème fraîche
2 tablespoons Dijon mustard
2 teaspoons caster sugar
6 tablespoons chopped fresh dill
sea salt and freshly ground black pepper
sprigs of dill and curly endive, to serve

Serves 6

To make the gravad lax, mix the salt, sugar, peppercorns and dill in a bowl. Sprinkle a third of this mixture down the middle of three large pieces of foil. Put a fish fillet on top of the herbs, skin side down, then sprinkle with a third of the herb mixture. Put a second fillet on top of each one, skin side up. Sprinkle with the remaining herbs and fold over the foil to enclose the fish completely.

Put the packages on a deep-sided tray, with a board or a second tray on top, then weigh down with heavy food cans or weights. Marinate in the refrigerator for 24–36 hours.

When ready to serve, gently wash off the herb mixture and pat dry. Cut into slices slightly thicker than smoked salmon.

Mix all the ingredients for the dill cream in a bowl. Set aside.

To make the pancakes, boil and peel the potatoes, then mash through a mouli or potato ricer into a large bowl. Cool completely, then mash in the beaten eggs and flour. Beat in the milk, nutmeg and seasoning. Stir a third of the egg whites into the batter to loosen it, then fold in the rest.

Heat the oil or butter in a non-stick frying pan, and drop in spoonfuls of mixture. Cook 2–3 minutes until golden, turn over and cook for 2 minutes until golden. Serve the pancakes with the mackerel, dill cream, dill sprigs and curly endive.

gnocchi

potato gnocchi
with walnut and rocket pesto

The success of gnocchi depends on lightly mixing the potato and flour to the right consistency – smooth and slightly sticky. If you over-mix or are heavy handed, the gnocchi will be heavy too.

My friend's mother, who taught me this recipe, has a special secret ingredient – a slosh of grappa!

Serve the gnocchi with a tomato or meat sauce, or pesto made with basil, dried tomatoes, or this unusual combination.

750 g large floury potatoes, unpeeled
125 g plain flour, plus extra for rolling
salt, to taste

Rocket Pesto:
50 g trimmed rocket leaves, roughly chopped
25 g chopped walnuts
2 garlic cloves
125 ml extra-virgin olive oil
25 g freshly grated Parmesan cheese, plus extra, to serve
sea salt and freshly ground black pepper

Serves 4

1 To make the pesto, put the rocket, walnuts and garlic in a blender or food processor and process until finely chopped. Add the olive oil and blend well to form a purée.

2 Scrape the mixture into a bowl and stir in the Parmesan. Taste and adjust the seasoning with salt and freshly ground black pepper. Set aside to develop the flavours while you make the gnocchi.

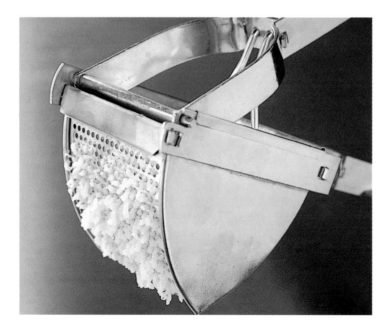

3 Put the potatoes in a pan with cold salted water to cover. Bring to the boil and cook for 25–30 minutes, until soft. Drain well, cool, then peel. While still warm, press through a potato ricer or mouli into a bowl.

4 Beat the flour into the potatoes, a little at a time. Stop adding flour when the mixture is smooth and slightly sticky (the moisture in the potatoes will vary according to their age and variety). Season with salt to taste.

5 Turn out the mixture onto a well-floured board, then roll out the dough into long sausages about 1 cm in diameter. Cut each sausage into short pieces about 2 cm long.

6 Place each piece on the end of your thumb and press the prongs of a fork lightly over the top. The pieces will be hollow on one side and grooved on the other. Drop them onto a floured plate as you make them.

7 Add 20–25 pieces at a time to a large pan of boiling water. They will quickly rise to the surface. Let them cook for 10–15 seconds more, then remove with a slotted spoon or strainer and put in a bowl while you cook the rest.

8 Add the pesto to the bowl and gently turn the gnocchi in the mixture, until they are well covered. Take care not to break them. Serve immediately with extra Parmesan cheese.

POTATO GNOCCHI **51**

The idea for this recipe comes from my Italian friend Daniela and is simply delicious. It is *pizza al trancio,* the Italian takeaway snack usually found in bakeries where slices are heated up for you (*trancio* means 'slice'). One slice is placed on top of the other with the filling in the middle, and then eaten like a sandwich.

pizza con le patate

Pizza Dough:

15 g fresh yeast, 1 tablespoon dried active yeast or 1 sachet easy-blend yeast

a pinch of sugar

200 ml warm water

375 g strong white bread flour

2 tablespoons olive oil

½ teaspoon salt

Herby Potato Topping:

500 g waxy potatoes, peeled and sliced thinly

2 tablespoon extra-virgin olive oil

4 garlic cloves, crushed

leaves from 2 sprigs of rosemary

1 teaspoon sea salt flakes

Makes two 23–25 cm pizzas

To make the pizza dough, put the fresh yeast, if using, and sugar in a small bowl and blend together well. Mix in the warm water and leave for 10 minutes or until frothy. For other yeasts follow the packet instructions.

Sieve the flour into a large bowl and make a well in the centre. Pour in the yeast mixture with the olive oil and salt. Mix together to form a soft but firm dough. Turn out onto a lightly floured surface and knead the dough for 10 minutes until smooth.

Divide the dough in half and form into balls. Put the dough balls on a floured work surface or tray in a warm place and sprinkle them liberally with flour. (This will become the base of the pizza and make it easier to slide onto the tray.) Let rise for about 1 hour or until doubled in size.

Put 2 baking sheets in a preheated oven at 220°C (425°F) Gas Mark 7 until hot. Put the potato slices, olive oil, garlic, rosemary and salt into a large bowl and toss together to coat.

Brush off any excess flour from the top of the dough, then turn the balls upside down on a work surface and roll and pull each one out to a large circle about 23–25 cm diameter. Spread the potato mixture evenly over both pizzas. Remove the trays from the oven and slide 1 pizza onto each one. Sprinkle with more olive oil and salt if required and bake for 15–20 minutes until the potatoes are tender and the pizzas lightly golden and crisp.

rösti

swiss rösti

A Swiss classic. I once worked as a chef in Switzerland, and I cooked rösti hundreds of times. These soft buttery pancakes topped with wild mushrooms are reminiscent of a dish I tasted one summer high in the Alps. My friend Stephan has an 84-year-old grandmother who picked the wild mushrooms from the forests in the surrounding valleys. Rösti can also be served topped with fried eggs, sprinkled with Gruyère cheese or served separately with meat and sausages.

1 kg potatoes, unpeeled and well scrubbed
175 g clarified butter *
1 onion, chopped
125 g pancetta or streaky bacon, cut into thin strips
500 g wild or flat field mushrooms, or a mixture of both, cut in halves or quarters if large
2 tablespoons chopped fresh flat-leaf parsley
sea salt and freshly ground black pepper
Serves 4

*To clarify butter, melt over a gentle heat, then let cool. Skim off the pure butter and discard the solids and water.

1 Put the whole potatoes in a large pan and cover with cold water. Bring to the boil and cook for 10–15 minutes until just tender. Drain well, let cool slightly, peel, then grate coarsely into a large bowl.

2 Heat 2 tablespoons of the butter in a frying pan, add the onion and bacon and cook for 5–6 minutes until the onions are softened. Tip this mixture into the bowl of potato, season with salt and pepper and mix well.

3 Heat half the remaining butter in a pan, add the potato mixture and press down slightly to form a large pancake. Cook for 10 minutes, adding a little extra butter around the edges and shaking the pan occasionally.

4 Carefully cover the pan with a plate and flip over. Add more butter, then slide the rösti back in to cook the other side. Add butter around the edge and cook until golden, about 7 minutes. Remove from the heat and keep warm.

5 Heat the remaining butter in a frying pan. Add the mushrooms and cook, stirring occasionally, for 3–5 minutes until tender but still firm. Season with salt and pepper and stir in the chopped parsley.

6 Serve the rösti topped with the mushrooms. You can also divide the rösti mixture in 4 before cooking to serve as a small starter – or vary the topping according to taste, and garnish with a few peppery salad leaves.

This method of cracking the potatoes and cooking them in wine comes from Cyprus. Cooked slowly with coriander seeds, the potatoes absorb all the lovely juices.

patates spastes

cracked new potatoes
in coriander and red wine

1 kg small new potatoes, unpeeled, scrubbed and dried

4 tablespoons olive oil

1 tablespoon coriander seeds, crushed well

150 ml red wine

4 tablespoons chopped fresh coriander leaves

salt and pepper

Serves 4–6

Put the potatoes in a clean cloth and, using a wooden mallet or other heavy kitchen implement, thump the potatoes to crack them open. (Don't be over-zealous or you will end up with raw mashed potato!)

Gently heat the oil in a pan large enough to hold the potatoes in a single layer. Add the potatoes, coriander seeds, salt and pepper and cook, turning the potatoes occasionally until lightly golden all over. Add the wine, let it boil, then reduce the heat, cover the pan and simmer gently, shaking the pan occasionally, for 15–20 minutes or until the potatoes are tender.

Remove from the heat and stir in the chopped fresh coriander leaves. Serve as an accompaniment to meat or poultry.

A wonderful creamy gratin of waxy potatoes layered with spinach, herbs, Gruyère and crème fraîche. It can be served hot or cold and would make an easily transportable picnic dish.

potato gratin
with herbs, spinach and cheese

1 garlic clove, crushed

15 g unsalted butter, melted

500 g trimmed fresh spinach

3 eggs, beaten

500 g crème fraîche

125 g grated Gruyère cheese

50 g chopped fresh herbs, such as chives, parsley, chervil or sorrel

a pinch of freshly grated nutmeg

a pinch of cayenne pepper

1.25 kg large waxy potatoes, peeled and thinly sliced

salt and freshly ground black pepper

To Serve:

salad leaves, such as shin joi, red chicory (endive) or red shiso

vinaigrette

sea salt

cracked black pepper

Serves 6-8

Mix the garlic and melted butter together and use to grease a deep 23 cm springform cake tin.

Wash the spinach and put in a large pan with just the water that is left clinging to the leaves. Cover and cook, stirring once, until the spinach has just wilted. Drain well and squeeze out any excess moisture. Chop finely.

Beat the eggs with the crème fraîche, stir in the chopped cooked spinach and two-thirds of the Gruyère. Add the herbs and season well with nutmeg, cayenne, salt and pepper. Slice the potatoes thinly.

Cover the base of the cake tin with a layer of potatoes and spread evenly with a spoonful of the cream and spinach mixture. Continue layering, finishing with a layer of potatoes. Sprinkle with the remaining Gruyère cheese and herbs, then cover the tin with a piece of foil.

Put the filled cake tin in a roasting tin and pour around enough boiling water to come half way up the sides. Carefully put in a preheated oven and cook at 180°C (350°F) Gas Mark 4 for about 1½ hours or until the potatoes are tender – test by piercing the centre with a knife or skewer. Remove the foil for the last 15 minutes to allow the top to brown.

Turn out onto a plate and serve hot or cold with salad leaves drizzled with vinaigrette and sprinkled with sea salt and lots of cracked black pepper.

potato soufflé
with mozzarella and almond-parsley pesto

Each spring, summer and autumn, I teach at the excellent Tasting Places cookery school in Sicily, and was shown this Italian recipe by Carla Tomasi, one of my fellow chefs at the school.

A soufflé of hot fluffy potato with nuggets of mozzarella and fontina cheese melting delectably through the mixture – it is the epitome of comfort food.

Serve the soufflé with this wonderfully scented pesto of roasted almonds and parsley puréed with the finest extra-virgin olive oil for a perfect accompaniment to salad as a lunch or supper dish.

50 g unsalted butter, melted

50 g dry breadcrumbs

1.5 kg floury potatoes, unpeeled, boiled in lightly salted water for 30 minutes, or until very soft, then drained and peeled while still hot

50 g unsalted butter, at room temperature

150 ml milk, warmed

2 eggs, plus 1 egg yolk

50 g freshly grated Parmesan cheese

1 mozzarella cheese, about 125 g, well drained and cubed

125 g fontina or Emmental cheese, cubed

Almond Parsley Pesto:

1 bunch of flat-leaf parsley, washed and stalks removed

50 g almonds with skin on, toasted in the oven until very golden, then cooled

250 ml extra-virgin olive oil

75 g Parmesan cheese, grated

salt and freshly ground black pepper

Serves 4

1 Grind the parsley, toasted almonds and 2 tablespoons olive oil to a fairly rough texture in a mortar and pestle or food processor. Scrape into a bowl, then stir in the remaining oil and Parmesan cheese and season to taste.

2 Before making the the soufflé, generously grease a 23 cm soufflé dish or cake tin with half the melted butter, then coat well with half the breadcrumbs, shaking out any excess.

3 Mash the hot potatoes through a potato ricer or mouli, or push through a sieve. Add the butter and warm milk and mix well. Beat the eggs, add to the mixture and season well. Add the Parmesan and mix well again.

4 Spoon half the potato mixture into the prepared soufflé dish or tin, pushing it up against the sides. Drop in the cheese cubes, spreading them out slightly, then cover with the remaining potato mixture.

5 Brush with the remaining butter and sprinkle with breadcrumbs. Cook in a preheated oven at 180°C (350°F) Gas Mark 4 for 20 minutes, then increase to 220°C (425°F) Gas Mark 7 for 10 minutes until the top crust is golden.

6 Serve from the dish or spoon onto a serving plate, with salad and pesto. **Note:** The uncooked soufflé can be prepared 2 days in advance and refrigerated in its dish, but bring back to room temperature before baking.

When mixed with wheat flour, or even made into potato flour, potatoes produce wonderful texture in baked goods. Pastry made with potato, for instance, is light and crumbly, potato bread has a delicious moist crumb, and shortbread made with a percentage of potato flour has a fine texture.

kartoffelkrapfen

potato turnovers
with chicken livers

1 kg floury potatoes, unpeeled

50 g unsalted butter

150 g self-raising flour

1 teaspoon caraway seeds

1 egg, beaten

Chicken Liver Filling:

50 g unsalted butter

1 onion, finely chopped

1 celery stalk, finely chopped

1 carrot, finely chopped

500 g chicken livers, trimmed

½ teaspoon paprika

1 tablespoon tomato purée

125 ml white wine or chicken stock

4 tablespoons chopped fresh parsley

salt and freshly ground black pepper

To Coat:

1 egg, beaten

50 g fine dry breadcrumbs

Makes 16–18

Put the potatoes in a pan of salted water, bring to the boil and simmer for about 30 minutes or until soft. Peel the potatoes while still warm and pass through a potato ricer or mouli, or push through a sieve into a large bowl. Beat in the butter, egg, salt and pepper, then gradually knead in the flour and caraway seeds until well mixed. Tip onto a well-floured work surface and roll out to 5 mm thick. Let cool completely.

To prepare the filling, melt the butter in a frying pan. Add the onion, celery and carrot and cook until softened and lightly golden. Raise the heat, add the chicken livers and cook, stirring frequently, until sealed all over. Stir in the paprika, tomato purée and wine or stock. Stir in the chopped parsley, season with salt and pepper and let cool.

Cut the potato dough into rounds 12 cm in diameter and put 1 tablespoon of filling in the centre. Fold over and press the edges firmly together. Put on a greased baking sheet, brush with the remaining egg, sprinkle with breadcrumbs and cook in a preheated oven at 200°C (400°F) Gas Mark 6 for 20–30 minutes until golden. Serve as a snack, or a light lunch with salad.

Salt cod is a traditional export from Scandinavia to Catholic Europe and even to the Caribbean. It appears, with potatoes, in the dishes of many countries, from the *brandade* of France to the baccalá of Venice.

portuguese fish fritters
with Greek skorthalia

500 g salt cod fillets

500 g floury potatoes, unpeeled, scrubbed well

1 small onion, finely chopped

2 tablespoons chopped fresh flat-leaf parsley

1 egg, lightly beaten

freshly ground nutmeg

salt and freshly ground black pepper

50 g flour, for coating

vegetable oil, for deep-frying

Greek Skorthalia:

50 g fresh white breadcrumbs

75 g ground almonds

4 garlic cloves, crushed

1–2 tablespoons freshly squeezed lemon juice

150 ml extra-virgin olive oil

salt and freshly ground black pepper

Makes 32

Put the fish in a bowl of water and chill for 24 to 36 hours, changing the water 2–3 times. Drain, rinse and put in a pan of cold water. Bring to the boil, then simmer for 5–10 minutes until tender. Drain, cool a little, remove the skin and bones, then flake the flesh into a bowl and mash with a fork.

Cook the potatoes in a large pan of salted water for 15 minutes until just tender. (Do not test before this time or the potatoes will be very soggy.) Drain, cool a little, then peel and mash the flesh well, preferably with a mouli or potato ricer.

Mix the potatoes into the fish, then add the onion, parsley, egg, nutmeg and pepper. Taste and add salt if needed. Divide into 32 walnut-sized balls, put on a tray, cover and chill for 30 minutes. Sprinkle the flour on a large plate. Roll each fish ball lightly into the flour, shaking off any excess, then set aside.

To make the skorthalia, put the breadcrumbs in a bowl, cover with water, soak for 5 minutes, then squeeze out the excess liquid. Put in a blender or food processor, add the almonds, garlic and 1 tablespoon lemon juice. Process briefly until mixed. With the motor running, gradually add the olive oil in a very thin steady stream until the mixture resembles mayonnaise. Scrape into a bowl and season with salt, pepper and more lemon juice to taste. Heat the oil in a deep pan to 190°C(375°F) or until a cube of bread browns in 40 seconds. Add the fish balls a few at a time and deep-fry for about 2 minutes turning occasionally until golden all over and cooked through. Serve hot with the skorthalia.

Potatoes thrive in cold climates, and Scandinavia is the source of many great potato dishes. This is the classic Swedish gratin of potato, anchovies and onions baked in cream. Nobody seems to know who the legendary Jansson was, or why he was tempted, but this recipe is so delicious it's no wonder he succumbed!

jansson's frestelse

jansson's temptation

50 g unsalted butter

2 large onions, thinly sliced

1 kg waxy potatoes, peeled

16–24 anchovy fillets in olive oil *

450 ml single cream

sea salt and freshly ground black pepper

Serves 4

*If possible, use the less salty Swedish anchovies, or white anchovies, usually sold in jars.

Grease a gratin dish with a little of the butter. Melt half the remaining butter in a pan, add the onions and cook for about 10 minutes or until softened and lightly golden.

Cut the potatoes into matchstick-sized pieces – this is easiest using a mandolin, but otherwise use the small cutting disc on a food processor, or simply cut with a knife.

Layer the potatoes, onions and anchovies into the gratin dish, starting and ending with potatoes. Criss-cross the anchovies as you go and season between the layers.

Dot with the remaining butter and put in a preheated oven 190°C (375°F) Gas Mark 5 for 10 minutes. Remove from the oven, pour over half the cream and return to the oven for a further 10 minutes. Pour over the remaining cream and cook for about 20–30 minutes or until the potatoes are tender and golden brown.

Hasselbacks are perhaps the best-known of all Swedish potato recipes. The original uses butter and breadcrumbs, and sometimes Parmesan, and bay leaves are a favourite Scandinavian herb. The potatoes are sliced almost to the base, so the slices open out like a fan when cooked, and the edges become crispy and golden.

hasselbackpotatis

bay-roasted hasselbacks

24 small potatoes, unpeeled, well scrubbed
approximately 20 fresh bay leaves, torn in half lengthways
15 g unsalted butter
3 tablespoons olive oil
1–2 garlic cloves, crushed
sea salt flakes and
freshly ground black pepper

Serves 4–6

To prepare the potatoes, place 2 chopsticks on a board and lay a potato lengthways between them. Using a sharp knife, and holding the sticks and potato in place, make crossways cuts 3 mm apart, cutting just down to the sticks. Alternatively, spear each potato with a skewer about 5 mm from the base, slice across as described above, then remove the skewer.

Insert a couple of pieces of bay leaf, or a whole leaf if small, in each sliced potato. Melt the butter with the olive oil in a heavy-based roasting tin. Over moderate heat, stir in the garlic and carefully add the potatoes in a single layer. (Take care, or they may sputter.) Move them around for 2–3 minutes to colour slightly, then season with freshly ground black pepper and sea salt flakes. Put the tin in a preheated oven at 190°C (375°F) Gas Mark 5 and roast for 25–30 minutes until golden brown and tender. As they cook, the potatoes will open out like a fan.

Serve as accompaniment to meat or poultry, or with fish such as baked cod or roasted salmon.

Pure comfort food, champ and colcannon are an inextricable part of Irish childhood memories. Dip each forkful of potato in the little pool of butter before eating. Blue cheese, especially Irish Cashel Blue, is my own optional addition!

champ

750 g floury potatoes, peeled

a bunch of spring onions, including the green tops, chopped

300 ml milk

50 g butter, plus extra for serving

175 g blue cheese, crumbled (optional)

salt and freshly ground black pepper

Serves 4

Cut the potatoes into large, even dice and cook in boiling salted water for 20–25 minutes or until tender. Drain well. Put the spring onions in a saucepan with the milk, bring to the boil, then simmer for 2–3 minutes. Remove from the heat and infuse for 10 minutes.

Mash the potatoes using a potato ricer or mouli, beat in the milk and spring onion mixture, then the butter, salt and pepper. Put in a clean pan and reheat.

To serve, spoon into small bowls in mounds, make a hollow in the top and insert more butter and cheese (if using).

Variations:

Colcannon (shown left), Ireland

Kale, cabbage or other leafy green vegetable is used instead of the spring onion and cheese. It is served in the same way as champ, or formed into little cakes and fried in butter to form a crunchy crust.

Clapshot, Scotland

Follow the recipe for champ. Omit the cheese and add 750 g mashed swedes. Chives or bacon fat may also be added. The chopped spring onions are optional.

Kailkenny, Scottish Highlands

Follow the recipe for colcannon, adding 125 ml cream.

Rumbledethumps, Scottish Borders

750 g each of cooked potatoes and cabbage are thumped (mashed) then rumbled (mixed) with pepper and 125 g butter, topped with cheese and grilled until brown.

Punchnep, Wales

Half-and-half mashed turnips (neps) and potatoes are heaped into a mound and studded with hollows, which are then filled with cream.

champ

potatoes dauphinoise

Two of the finest French potato dishes are *gratin dauphinois* and *pommes à la dauphinoise*. They are very similar, but in the latter, sliced potatoes are baked with cream and garlic. (I prefer to roast or boil the garlic first, for a more subtle flavour, but use crushed raw garlic if you prefer.) To make *gratin dauphinois* pour a mixture of eggs, milk and cream over the potatoes, then top with cheese before baking. The two names refer to the eastern French province of Dauphiné, stretching from Savoy to Provence, rather than the *Dauphine*, the wife of the former French crown prince (the *Dauphin*).

4 garlic cloves
450 ml double cream
200 ml milk
1 kg floury potatoes, peeled
sea salt and
freshly ground white pepper
butter, for greasing
Serves 4

pommes à la dauphinoise

1 Drop the garlic into a small pan of boiling water, reduce the heat and simmer for 20 minutes until very tender. Remove, then crush well to a purée using a mortar and pestle, or press through a fine sieve.

2 Put the puréed garlic in a saucepan with the milk and cream, season very well, bring to the boil, then remove from the heat.

3 Grease a roasting tin or dish measuring about 25 x 15 cm or round cake tin, about 23 cm diameter. Slice the peeled potatoes into 5 mm slices and arrange in the pan in 6 or 7 layers.

4 Pour over the cream and press the potatoes down. The cream should come just under the top layer. Cook in a preheated oven at 160°C (325°F) Gas Mark 3 for 1½–2 hours, pressing the potatoes down gently every 20 minutes.

5 The cream will be absorbed gradually and the potatoes will become compressed and more solid as they cook. If there appears to be too much liquid, remove some with a spoon. When the top is coloured, stop pressing.

6 Test with a knife to check if the potatoes are cooked. Remove from the oven and let rest in a warm place for 10 minutes. Spoon straight from the dish or cut out shapes with pastry cutters for a more elegant serving.

This is a variation on the French classic potato dish *Pommes Anna* – the potato cooks down to form a solid cake that melts in the mouth. When I first worked as a chef, I used a traditional copper *Pommes Anna* mould, but I find that an ovenproof cast-iron frying pan or cake tin works just as well.

pommes voisin

1 kg waxy potatoes, peeled
75 g melted butter
25 g freshly grated Parmesan cheese
sprigs of thyme, to serve (optional)
sea salt and freshly ground black pepper
Serves 4

Variations:
Pommes Voisin with Jerusalem Artichokes
add to the above ingredients:
375 g Jerusalem artichokes
juice of 1 lemon
Pommes Anna
ingredients as for Pommes Voisin,
omitting the Parmesan cheese.

Slice the peeled potatoes finely into rounds about 1 mm thick (slicing on a mandolin is easiest).

Generously butter a 15 cm round cake tin and arrange a layer of potatoes in a circle over the base, neatly overlapping each slice. Drizzle with a little of the melted butter, sprinkle with some of the Parmesan and season with salt and pepper. Continue layering, drizzling with butter, sprinkling with cheese and seasoning, until all the potatoes have been used. Drizzle the remaining butter over the top and cook in a preheated oven at 220°C (425°F) Gas Mark 7 for about 40–50 minutes or until very tender. Press down the potato slices 3–4 times during baking to form a solid cake.

Variations:

Pommes Voisin with Jerusalem Artichokes

Peel and slice the artichokes in the same way as the potatoes, dropping them into a bowl of water acidulated with the lemon juice to prevent discolouration. Drain and pat dry just before using. Alternate layers of artichokes with layers of potato and proceed as in the main recipe.

Pommes Anna

Follow the main recipe, omitting the Parmesan cheese.

potato noodles
with red cherry compote

These noodles are not long and thin as one might think, but rather little fried squares of potato and semolina served either savoury or sweet. This sweet cherry compote is based on an original German recipe.

Put the potatoes in a saucepan, cover with cold water, bring to the boil, then simmer for 25–30 minutes until tender. When cool enough to handle, peel and pass through a potato ricer or mouli into a clean saucepan.

Put the saucepan on the heat and gradually whisk in the milk until smooth. Cook, whisking continuously (do not allow to catch or burn) until it starts to boil. Sprinkle in the semolina in a thin stream, whisking all the time. Continue cooking until the mixture thickens. Remove from the heat and beat in the eggs. Spread onto a lightly greased Swiss roll tin 33 x 22 x 1.5 cm, smoothing the surface. Let cool completely. Turn the mixture out onto a work surface and cut into 2.5 cm strips. Cut across again into small squares or diamonds.

To make the compote, put the cherries in a saucepan with the sugar, orange zest and juice. Stir well, bring to the boil, reduce the heat, cover and simmer for 5–10 minutes or until the cherries are tender. Remove from the heat and stir in the Kirsch. Set aside.

Put the sugar and cinnamon in a pan, heat well and stir, then transfer to a large plate or tray.

Melt the butter in a large frying pan and cook the potato squares until lightly golden on both sides. Drain well on kitchen paper then transfer them to the tray of cinnamon sugar and toss well to coat, shaking off any excess. Serve with sour cream and the warm compote, scattered with the toasted almonds.

500 g floury potatoes, unpeeled

600 ml milk

75 g fine semolina

2 eggs, beaten

75 g caster sugar

½ teaspoon ground cinnamon

75 g butter

Red Cherry Compote:

500 g sweet red cherries, stoned

25 g caster sugar

1 strip of orange zest

juice of 1 orange

2 tablespoons Kirsch

50 g flaked almonds, toasted

sour cream, to serve

Serves 4

kartoffelnudeln

An updated version of a traditional, old-fashioned bread. Potato and potato flour produce bread with a moist texture that keeps well and is very good toasted. Potato flour has no gluten, so whenever it is used alone in recipes, it is suitable for people on gluten-free diets.

honey potato bread
with saffron and a poppyseed glaze

250 g floury potatoes, peeled

a large pinch of saffron strands

425 g bread flour

I teaspoon salt

I½ teaspoons easy-blend dry yeast

2 tablespoons honey

75 g unsalted butter, melted

2 egg yolks, beaten

125 g raisins

Poppyseed Glaze:

I egg white, beaten

I tablespoon black poppyseeds

Makes 2 loaves

Add the potatoes to a pan of boiling water, reduce the heat and simmer until tender. Drain, reserving 250 ml of the cooking water in a bowl, then steep the saffron strands in the bowl for 30 minutes.

Press the drained potatoes through a potato ricer, mouli or fine sieve into a large bowl. Add the reserved potato water and saffron and mix together well.

Sieve the flour and salt into a large bowl and stir in the dried yeast. Add the potato mixture, honey, butter, egg yolks and raisins and mix well to form a soft but firm dough.

Turn the dough onto a floured work surface and knead well for 10 minutes. Tip into an oiled bowl or oiled polythene bag, cover the bowl or tie the bag and leave in a warm place for about 1–1½ hours or until doubled in size.

Turn the dough onto a floured work surface, punch down and knead well for a further 5 minutes. Cut in half and form into 2 round loaves. Put on 2 greased baking sheets and score each loaf with a knife in a criss-cross pattern. Cover loosely and let rise again for 45 minutes to 1 hour, until doubled in size.

Brush with egg white and sprinkle with poppyseeds. Cook in a preheated oven at 200°C (400°F) Gas Mark 6 for 40 minutes or until the bottom sounds hollow when tapped. Cool on a wire rack and eat within 5 days or freeze for up to 1 month.

Scottish cooks are famous around the world for their baking skills, and scones are perhaps their finest achievement. Scottish scones are cooked with many different flavourings, but the Parmesan cheese and pancetta used in this recipe reflect the influence of the large Italian-Scottish community living 'north of the border'. Mashed potato is used to replace some of the flour, giving a light, moist texture.

golden potato scones
with parmesan and pancetta

4 slices pancetta or bacon, about 50 g, cut into small pieces

150–175 g plain flour

2 teaspoons baking powder

½ teaspoon salt, cut into small pieces

50 g unsalted butter, diced

125 g cooked mashed potato

50 g Parmesan cheese, cut into tiny cubes

1 teaspoon dried oregano

about 2 tablespoons milk

1 egg yolk, beaten, to glaze

Makes 10

Heat a frying pan without oil and dry-fry the pancetta or bacon for 5–6 minutes or until crispy. Remove with a slotted spoon and let cool on kitchen paper.

Sieve the flour, baking powder and salt together into a large bowl. Add the butter and rub in until the mixture resembles breadcrumbs. Add the potato, Parmesan, oregano and cooked pancetta or bacon pieces and mix well. Add enough milk to form a soft but firm dough, turn out onto a lightly floured work surface and knead briefly. Roll out the dough to 1.5 cm thick and, using a fluted cutter, stamp out 6 cm rounds. Re-roll any trimmings and cut more rounds, to make about 10 in total.

Place the scones on a well-greased baking sheet, brush the tops with the beaten egg and cook in a preheated oven at 220°C (425°F) Gas Mark 7 for 10–15 minutes or until golden brown and well risen. Cool a little on a wire rack, then serve while still warm, spread with unsalted butter.

the middle east

The precise date of the potato's adoption into the cuisines of the Middle East cannot be pinpointed. However the **sophisticated spicing** typical of the dishes from this region is perfectly suited to the flavour-absorbing properties of the potato.

This recipe is based on a Persian potato omelette but with broad beans added. Use frozen broad beans if you can't find fresh ones – the broad bean is one of the few foods that is almost as good frozen as fresh. Frozen ones are also easier to pop out of their little grey coats, leaving the brilliant green bean behind. This dish is good as a starter or served with drinks.

kuku sibzamini

kuku sibzamini

250 g broad beans, podded if fresh, defrosted if frozen

500 g cooked potatoes, mashed

6 eggs, beaten

1 teaspoon ground turmeric

6 spring onions, chopped

2 tablespoons chopped fresh coriander

1 tablespoon chopped fresh flat-leaf parsley

25 g unsalted butter

salt and freshly ground black pepper

Serves 6–8 as a starter

If using fresh broad beans, blanch them in lightly salted boiling water for 4 minutes, then drain, refresh in cold water, then drain again. Pop the fresh or frozen broad beans out of their skins and set aside. (Discard the skins.)

Place the cooked, mashed potato in a large bowl, then stir in the beaten eggs and ground turmeric. Fold in the broad beans, spring onions and herbs, then season with salt and black pepper.

Put the butter in a heavy-based non-stick frying pan with a heatproof handle, and melt over moderate heat. Pour in the potato mixture. Reduce the heat to very low and cook without stirring for 15–20 minutes or until the eggs have set and the base is golden brown (check by lifting the edge with a palette knife).

Put the pan under a grill to brown the top of the omelette, then slide the omelette onto a large plate or tray and cut into small squares or wedges. Serve hot or cold.

The potato is known as *batata* in Arabic. This salad from Saudi Arabia combines a traditional Middle Eastern ingredient, the chickpea, with the more recent arrival, the potato. As carbohydrates packed full of fibre, both are particularly good for absorbing the spicy, sophisticated flavours typical of Middle Eastern food.

sultan's salad

125 g dried chickpeas

1–2 garlic cloves, chopped

50 g shelled walnuts

4 tablespoons chopped fresh flat-leaf parsley

2 tablespoons chopped fresh mint

4 tablespoons tahini paste

4–5 tablespoons freshly squeezed lemon juice

75 ml extra-virgin olive oil

about 75 ml water

750 g unpeeled new or waxy potatoes

a pinch of paprika

sea salt

To Serve (optional):

2 tablespoons chopped walnuts

1 tablespoon toasted sesame seeds

4 sprigs of mint

Serves 4

Put the chickpeas in a bowl, cover with cold water and let soak overnight.

Next day, drain the chickpeas and rinse well. Put in a pan of cold water (do not add salt as this will make the chickpeas tough), bring to the boil, reduce the heat and simmer for 50 minutes to 1 hour or until tender.

Drain well and reserve in a large bowl.

Put the garlic, walnuts and herbs in the bowl of a food processor or blender. Pulse until finely chopped. Add the tahini paste and 4 tablespoons of the lemon juice and whizz to mix. With the motor running, add the olive oil in a thin steady stream until amalgamated. Add enough water to make a thin dressing.

Pour the sauce into a bowl and season to taste with salt, paprika and more lemon juice if needed.

Add the potatoes to a saucepan of lightly salted boiling water and simmer for 15–20 minutes or until tender. Drain well, then cut the potatoes in half and add to the bowl with the chickpeas.

Pour over the dressing and toss well while still warm.

Serve warm or cold sprinkled with chopped walnuts, toasted sesame seeds and sprigs of fresh mint leaves.

I was taught this recipe by the mother of Marwan Badran, a London-based Iraqi friend. Iraqi Seville oranges are sweeter than most, so after much testing of this recipe, the Badrans, *mère et fils*, found that substituting oranges and lemons produces the right balance of sweetness and sharpness. It is a wonderful, yellow-orange stew, heavily-scented with all the spices of the Middle East.

chicken potato stew
with 'Seville' oranges

a large pinch of saffron strands

2 tablespoons olive oil

1 whole chicken, about 2 kg, cut into 8 pieces

2 tablespoons plain flour

1 teaspoon salt, plus extra to taste

crushed black seeds from 6 green cardamom pods

1 teaspoon whole cloves

1 teaspoon allspice berries

1 teaspoon whole black peppercorns

1 teaspoon whole pink peppercorns

2 cinnamon sticks, 7 cm each

juice of 2 large oranges

juice of 2 large lemons

750 g floury potatoes, peeled and cut into large 7 cm chunks

1 whole lemon, sliced

1 whole orange, sliced

1–2 tablespoons rosewater

Serves 4

Put the saffron strands in a small heatproof bowl and pour over the boiling water. Leave to infuse.

Heat the olive oil in a large casserole and fry the chicken, about 2 or 3 pieces at a time, until lightly golden all over. Remove the pieces to a tray as they are sealed. Drain off all but 1 tablespoon of the fat. Add the flour and cook for 1–2 minutes, then add the saffron and its infusing water. Stir well.

Add the chicken pieces to the pot, add the salt, spices, orange and lemon juices. Pour over enough water to cover (about 1.2 litres), and bring to the boil. Add the potato pieces and the slices of orange and lemon.

Reduce the heat to low, cover with a lid and simmer gently for 30–35 minutes or until tender, occasionally skimming off any fat that rises to the surface.

Taste and adjust the seasoning, then stir in rosewater to taste. Serve with rice.

potato chap

This is an Iraqi version of the Lebanese *kibbeh,* which are usually made with bulgar wheat instead of potato. For *chap*, cooked potato is mashed and formed into a thin shell by hand and filled with spiced minced meat. Making *chap* requires a little skilful artistry and a good *chap* maker is highly admired for her deft finger work in creating perfect little ovals or globes with tiny pinched ends. *Chap* and *kibbeh* are a very common form of street food in the Middle East, equivalent to spring rolls or sausage rolls. They can also be served as a snack, or for lunch squashed into pitta bread with salad and creamy tahini sauce.

1 kg floury potatoes, unpeeled, scrubbed well
1 tablespoon cornflour
1 teaspoon salt
1 egg, beaten
2 tablespoons fine dry breadcrumbs

Meat Filling:
2 tablespoons olive oil
1 large onion, finely chopped
50 g pine nuts
500 g minced lamb or beef
1½ teaspoons mixed spice
50 g raisins
4 tablespoons chopped fresh flat-leaf parsley
75 g fine dry breadcrumbs
salt and freshly ground black pepper
vegetable oil, for deep-frying

Makes 16

chap

1 Boil the potatoes in salted water for 15–20 minutes until tender (test after 15 minutes). Drain, then peel and pass through a potato ricer or mouli into a large bowl. Beat in the cornflour, salt and egg. Knead and mix in the breadcrumbs.

2 To make the filling, eat the oil in a heavy-based pan, add the onions and fry for 5–6 minutes until softened and translucent, add the pine nuts and cook for about 5 minutes until golden.

3 Add the meat, mixed spice, raisins and seasonings to the pan and cook for about 10–15 minutes until brown and no liquid remains. Stir in the parsley. Drain and pat the cooked mixture dry on kitchen paper.

4 Divide the potato mixture into 16 portions. Dip your hands in water and put one portion in your palm. Make an indentation with your thumb, and pinch the sides while turning the ball in your palm to form a thin, even shell.

5 Put 1 tablespoon of the cooked spiced meat mixture in the hole and smooth the sides of the pastry around the mixture.

6 Gradually pinch the opening closed and smooth it over, forming a flat oval and patting the surface until smooth. Patch any holes with a little extra potato mixture. Place on a tray and repeat with the remaining mixture.

7 Spread the breadcrumbs on a plate or tray and gently roll each oval *chap* in the breadcrumbs until evenly covered. Pat the breadcrumbs on gently so they stick well, then shake off any excess crumbs.

8 Heat the oil in a deep pan to 190°C (375°F) or until a cube of bread browns in 40 seconds. Deep-fry the *chap* in batches until cooked through and golden brown. Drain on kitchen paper and serve hot with pitta and salad.

Some **New World** vegetables, formerly thought to have been introduced to the rest of the world **after 1492**, may have been taken to Africa **much earlier**, by Arab seafarers in the middle of the **first millenium**. Potatoes may have reached Africa at that time.

africa

moroccan couscous

Couscous is the national dish of Morocco, traditionally made in a *couscousière*, a large, double-layered pot. It is much more easily made these days thanks to the advent of easy-cook couscous. I learned how to make this dish from a Moroccan chef I worked with in Switzerland, who cooked it as a treat for the staff. Recent scholarship suggests that it may have been Arab seafarers from the Atlantic coast of Morocco who brought New World ingredients to North and West Africa during medieval times, when Arab art and scholarship reached its zenith, and Europe was still mired in the Dark Ages.

125 g dried chickpeas, soaked
overnight in plenty of cold water

750 g lean shoulder or leg lamb,
cut into 3 cm pieces

2 onions, chopped

3 tablespoons olive oil

2 cinnamon sticks

½ teaspoon ground ginger

a large pinch of saffron strands

¼ teaspoon cayenne pepper
or chilli powder

3 turnips, halved or quartered if large

500 g small new potatoes, halved

250 g pumpkin, peeled and cubed

375 g shelled broad beans,
defrosted if frozen

250 g ripe tomatoes,
skinned, deseeded and chopped

500 g easy-cook couscous

75 g raisins

6 tablespoons chopped
fresh coriander leaves

75 g whole blanched almonds

3 tablespoons chopped
fresh flat-leaf parsley

50 g unsalted butter

salt and freshly ground black pepper

Serves 4

Drain and rinse the chickpeas and place in the bottom of a double boiler or *couscousière* with the lamb and onions. Add 2 tablespoons of the oil, the cinnamon, ginger, saffron and cayenne or chilli powder to the pot (do not add salt at this point or it will make the chickpeas tough). Cover with cold water (about 750 ml or enough just to cover).

Bring to the boil, reduce the heat, cover and simmer for 1 hour.

Add the turnips, potatoes, pumpkin, broad beans (if fresh) and the tomatoes, and continue cooking for a further 20 minutes.

Meanwhile, place the couscous in a large bowl and stir in hot water following the packet instructions. Leave for 15–20 minutes to allow the grains to swell, stirring occasionally with a fork to fluff up the grains.

Stir the broad beans (if frozen), raisins and coriander into the stew and season with salt and more pepper if needed. Add the prepared couscous to the top compartment of the *couscousière*. If using a double boiler with large holes in the top compartment, line with a layer of muslin over the holes before adding the couscous. Cover and cook for a further 20–30 minutes, fluffing up the grains occasionally with a fork.

Heat the remaining oil in a frying pan, add the blanched almonds and fry gently for 3–4 minutes or until golden brown. Stir the parsley into the stew, taste and adjust the seasoning. Tip the couscous into a large bowl and stir in the butter until melted, fluffing up the grains. Spoon the stew over the couscous and scatter with the toasted almonds.

Peanuts and plantains are widely used by cooks all over Sub-Saharan Africa, especially in West Africa. Though the potato is not indigenous to Africa, it is now used almost as much as its fellow imports, cassava and sweet potatoes, and native tubers, such as yams and taro. Variations of this soup can be made with any of these root vegetables.

potato peanut soup
with deep-fried plantain strips

3 tablespoons peanut (groundnut) oil

1 large onion, chopped

¼ teaspoon dried, crushed red chillies

4 medium tomatoes, skinned and chopped

500 g floury potatoes, peeled and cut into 2.5 cm cubes

150 g roasted, unsalted peanuts

1.2 litres chicken stock

sea salt, to season

To Serve:

1 plantain

vegetable oil, for deep-frying

50 g raw unsalted peanuts

a pinch of ground ginger

3 spring onions, finely chopped

Serves 4

Heat 2 tablespoons of the peanut oil in a large saucepan, add the onion and crushed red chillies and cook for 5–6 minutes or until the onion is softened and translucent but not coloured. Add the tomatoes, potatoes, peanuts and stock, season with salt and cook for 15–20 minutes or until the potato is very tender. Remove from the heat and purée in a blender or food processor, in batches if necessary, then strain through a sieve into a clean pan. To peel the plantain, make a slit with a small knife from the stalk down to the end, and run your thumb under the skin and peel it back. With a potato peeler, slice the plantain very thinly lengthways, then cut each slice into 5 mm strips. Heat the vegetable oil in a deep pan to 190°C (375°F), or until a cube of bread browns in 40 seconds. Deep-fry the plantain strips, a few at a time, until crisp and golden, then drain on kitchen paper.

Heat the remaining peanut oil in a frying pan over a low heat. Add the peanuts and cook for 1–2 minutes until just beginning to brown, then add a pinch of ground ginger and continue to cook until the peanuts are golden brown all over. Remove from the heat and scoop onto kitchen paper to drain.

Reheat the soup, season to taste and serve garnished with the plantain, peanuts and chopped spring onion.

The Portuguese introduced New World ingredients to Asia – and now it is impossible to think of **South-east Asian** food without chillies, or **Indian** cooking without potatoes (*aloo*) – so perfect with their **complex spice mixtures**.

asia

potato pakoras
with spicy tomato chutney

Pakoras are deep-fried Indian fritters made from potatoes or other vegetables dipped in chickpea flour batter. They are usually served with tea for lunch (tiffin), or as snacks or street foods at almost any time of the day. Nigella (*kalonji*) are black teardrop-shaped seeds with a peppery, lemon flavour and are often incorrectly sold as black onion seeds. Dried pomegranate seeds (*anardhana*) are used predominantly in North Indian cooking. They have a pleasant sweet-sour flavour and should be slightly sticky to the touch. Both spices are sold in Asian grocers and specialist delicatessens.

250 g gram (chickpea) flour

1 tablespoon dried
pomegranate seeds, ground

1 tablespoon nigella seeds

1 fresh green chilli, deseeded and
finely chopped

½ teaspoon ground turmeric

1 teaspoon ground cumin

1 teaspoon salt

200–250 ml water

500 g potatoes, peeled and cut into
5 mm slices

groundnut (peanut) or vegetable oil,
for deep-frying

Tomato Chutney:

1 kg ripe tomatoes,
skinned and chopped

1 large onion, chopped

2–3 garlic cloves, crushed

2.5 cm piece fresh ginger,
peeled and finely chopped

150 ml white wine vinegar

1 teaspoon salt

¼ teaspoon crushed dried red chillies

¼ teaspoon ground cloves

¼ teaspoon ground cardamon

¼ teaspoon ground cinnamon

200 g brown sugar

Serves 6 as a snack

To make the chutney, place the tomatoes, onion, garlic and ginger in a large heavy-based saucepan, stir to mix and cook over a medium heat for about 30 minutes until reduced to a thick pulp.

Reduce the heat to low and stir in the remaining ingredients. Cook, stirring occasionally (do not allow it to catch on the bottom), for about 30–40 minutes until fairly thick. Pour into a sterilized jar while still hot.

To make the pakoras, mix all the dry ingredients in a large bowl, then gradually mix in the water to make a fairly thick batter. Heat some oil in a deep pan to 190°C (375°F), or until a cube of bread browns in 40 seconds.

Dip the potato slices in the batter, add to the fat in batches and fry until golden brown all over, about 5–8 minutes. Drain on kitchen paper.

Serve hot with the tomato chutney or either of the variations below.

Variations:

Aubergine and Coriander Raita

Put a whole aubergine under a very hot grill or in a hot oven, and cook turning occasionally, until charred and very soft. Let cool, slit down the middle and squeeze to remove any bitter juices. Scoop out the flesh with a spoon into a bowl and mash well with a fork. Let cool completely. Add 300 ml plain yoghurt, 3 tablespoons chopped fresh coriander, season to taste with salt and pepper and serve sprinkled with garam masala.

Fresh Green Mint and Coriander Chutney

Put 6 tablespoons each of chopped fresh mint and fresh coriander leaves in a small food processor or spice grinder. Add 4 chopped green chillies (deseeded if preferred), 2 teaspoons sugar, 2 teaspoons garam masala, ½ teaspoon salt and 2 tablespoons fresh lemon juice. Add about 1–2 tablespoons cold water if needed and process until smooth. Scrape into a serving bowl, taste and add extra lemon juice if required.

roti

India has dozens of different kinds of bread – plain, flavoured with spices as here, or with spicy fillings. They are served with curry or dhaal, but these roti are made smaller to eat as a snack. Carry through the potato theme and serve roti with vodka-based drinks – vodka is sometimes made from potatoes, as well as from grains.

mini potato roti
with coconut and mint chutney

750 g large floury potatoes, peeled

2 fresh green chillies

½ teaspoon crushed dried red chillies

I small onion, finely chopped

I teaspoon salt

I teaspoon ground cumin

I teaspoon ground turmeric

2 tablespoons chopped
fresh coriander leaves

25 g unsalted butter, melted

150 g plain flour

vegetable oil, for frying

Coconut and Mint Chutney:

125 g grated fresh coconut or 75 g
unsweetened desiccated coconut

200 g plain yoghurt

I green chilli, deseeded and chopped

2 tablespoons chopped fresh mint

½ teaspoon salt

½ teaspoon sugar

Makes 64

If using desiccated coconut to make the chutney, put it in a bowl and cover with warm water. Let soak for about 20 minutes, then strain through a sieve, pressing the coconut against the sides of the sieve to squeeze out any excess moisture. Put all the chutney ingredients in a bowl, mix well and set aside.

Cook the potatoes in boiling salted water, drain and mash well. Deseed and finely chop the fresh chillies. Add to the potatoes and stir in all the remaining ingredients, except the flour, and mix well. Gradually mix in the flour until you have a soft dough. Divide the dough into equally sized pieces. Taking one piece at a time roll out on a floured board to a 7 cm circle. Continue with the remaining pieces of dough.

Heat a little oil in a heavy-based frying pan and cook the roti 2 or 3 at a time for 1–2 minutes on each side until lightly browned on each side. Serve with the coconut and mint chutney.

samosas

vegetable samosas

with potato and cauliflower

These crisp little triangular vegetable parcels are usually eaten as street food snacks and are found throughout India. Portuguese seafarers introduced New World ingredients such as chillies, peppers, corn and potatoes to India. The Portuguese were the earliest European traders in the area – a major mercantile power from Renaissance times and their influence persisted until they were forcibly ejected from the west-coast colony of Goa in the 1960s, almost twenty years after India gained independence in 1947.

Pastry:

300 g plain flour

½ teaspoon salt

4 tablespoons vegetable oil

8 tablespoons water

Cauliflower Potato Filling:

500 g floury potatoes, unpeeled and scrubbed

250 g small cauliflower florets

2 tablespoons vegetable oil

1 teaspoon black mustard seeds

1 onion, finely chopped

1 tablespoon finely grated fresh root ginger

1–2 green chillies, deseeded and very finely chopped

1 teaspoon ground coriander

½ teaspoon ground turmeric

1 teaspoon garam masala

½ teaspoon chilli powder

½ teaspoon salt

1–2 tablespoons lemon juice

3 tablespoons chopped fresh coriander leaves

vegetable oil, for deep-frying

Makes 18

1 To make the pastry, sift the flour and salt into a bowl, then rub in the oil. Gradually add water to make a firm dough, then turn onto a lightly floured surface. Knead 5 minutes until smooth, cover and let rest 30 minutes–1 hour.

2 Boil the potatoes in salted water for 15–20 minutes until just tender. Drain, peel and cut into 1 cm dice. Blanch the cauliflower florets briefly in boiling salted water, drain, refresh in plenty of cold water and drain again well.

3 Heat the oil in a pan, fry the mustard seeds until they pop, add the onions, ginger and chilli and cook for 5–6 minutes. Add the spices and salt and cook 1–2 minutes. Add the potatoes, cauliflower and 1 tablespoon lemon juice.

5 Cut a circle in half and brush the edges with water. Add 1 tablespoon filling and fold the pastry to form a cone. Press the straight edges to seal. Fold the rounded edges together and crimp to seal. Repeat with the remaining circles.

4 Cook for 2–3 minutes. Remove from the heat, add chopped coriander, salt and lemon juice to taste. Let cool. Divide the pastry into 9 balls. Work with one at a time, keeping the others covered, and roll into an 18 cm circle.

6 Heat the oil in a wide, deep pan to 190°C (375°F) or until a cube of bread browns in 40 seconds. Cook 2–3 samosas at a time for 4–5 minutes, turning once, until golden all over. Drain on kitchen paper and serve with chutney.

Popiah—delicious fillings wrapped in spring roll wrappers, ricepaper, or pancakes —are a popular snack food in Malaysia. Use this mixture of two flours to make the pancakes, or use plain flour only.

popiah
Malaysian popiah

150 g plain flour and 65 g rice flour

½ teaspoon salt

2 eggs, beaten

450 ml water

2 tablespoons vegetable oil,
plus extra for frying

Prawn and Ginger Filling:

175 g uncooked prawns, peeled

2 tablespoon vegetable oil

1 teaspoon finely grated ginger

2 garlic cloves, very thinly sliced

1 waxy potato, about 200 g,
peeled, grated and squeezed dry

1 medium carrot, grated

125 g mooli (white radish) grated

2½ tablespoons sweet yellow bean paste

6 spring onions, finely shredded

½ small cucumber, grated

200 g beansprouts

50 g firm bean curd (tofu), crumbled

6 red chillies, deseeded and well-crushed

12 crisp lettuce leaves

a small bunch of fresh coriander

soy sauce and sliced chilli, to serve

salt and freshly ground black pepper

Makes 12

To make the pancakes, sieve the flour/s and salt into a bowl. Make a well in the centre, add the eggs and whisk, adding enough water to make a thin batter. Strain through a sieve and stir in the oil. Let rest for 30 minutes before using.

To make the filling, devein and chop the prawns. Heat the oil in a frying pan, add the ginger and garlic and fry for 1–2 minutes until softened and golden. Add the prawns and fry for 1 minute. Add the grated potato, carrot and mooli and stir-fry for 1–2 minutes until just tender but still firm. Add the yellow bean paste and stir-fry for 1 minute. Remove from the heat and stir in the spring onion, cucumber, beansprouts and bean curd. Season to taste with salt and pepper and let cool.

Heat a non-stick crêpe or frying pan and add a little oil. Tip out any excess oil, then pour in a ladleful of the batter – enough to make a thin pancake. Swirl around to cover the base. Cook for 1–2 minutes until lightly browned, turn it over and cook the other side briefly. Repeat with the remaining batter to make 12 pancakes.

To assemble the popiah, spread each pancake with some chilli crushed to a paste, line with a lettuce leaf, and top with some of the cooked filling. Add a few coriander leaves, roll up tightly and cut into 2–3 slices. Alternatively, serve the filling ingredients separately for the guests to assemble themselves. Serve with a dip of soy sauce sprinkled with sliced red chilli.

kaeng kai

thai chicken curry
with potatoes and coconut milk

A delicious, very simple curry with all the flavours of Thailand. Fish sauce (*nam pla*) and delicious Thai curry pastes are available in South-east Asian stores. The curry pastes can be bought, ready-made, in either red, green, orange mussaman (Muslim), or paenang. The red paste is much more fiery than the green, while the mussaman paste is quite mild. Starchy foods like potatoes and rice have a particular affinity for the assertive spicy flavourings found in South-east Asia.

2 tablespoons vegetable oil

750 g boneless chicken (breasts or thighs), cut into large chunks

2–3 tablespoons red or green Thai curry paste

600 ml canned coconut milk

2½ tablespoons Thai fish sauce (*nam pla*)

2 tablespoons light brown sugar

500 g new potatoes, unpeeled, scrubbed and cut in half

½ teaspoon salt

1–2 tablespoons lime juice

To Serve:

50 g unsalted roasted peanuts

3 spring onions, cut into fine shreds and placed in a bowl of cold water

Thai basil or coriander, roughly chopped

2 kaffir lime leaves, finely sliced (optional)

Serves 4

1 Heat the vegetable oil in a large wok or frying pan, add the chicken pieces, in batches if necessary, and fry them briefly on all sides to seal. Remove the chicken pieces to a bowl.

2 Add the curry paste to the pan and stir-fry for about 30 seconds to release the aromas of the chillies and spices.

3 Add the coconut milk, fish sauce and sugar to the pan and stir well to mix. Return the sautéed chicken pieces to the pan, together with any juices that have accumulated in the bowl.

4 Bring the mixture to the boil, then add the potato halves and salt, and reduce the heat. Cover the pan and simmer for about 15–20 minutes until the chicken is cooked and the potatoes are tender.

5 Stir in the lime juice to taste and more salt if needed. Serve sprinkled with
the peanuts, spring onion strips, basil or coriander and the kaffir lime
strips, if using. Steamed jasmine rice is a suitable accompaniment.

The potato, known as *aloo* in several Indian languages, is an important ingredient for the large vegetarian Hindu population. It has revolutionized nutrition in high mountain areas, such as the Khumbu on the slopes of Everest, where the yield is more reliable than the grain crops it replaced.

Indian dry potato curry
in aubergine shells with yoghurt

2 large aubergines

750 g waxy potatoes, peeled and cut into 1 cm cubes

6–8 tablespoons vegetable oil

1 tablespoon cumin seeds

1 teaspoon black mustard seeds

1 teaspoon sesame seeds

1 onion, finely chopped

1–2 garlic cloves, crushed

1 teaspoon grated fresh ginger

1 fresh green chilli, deseeded and finely chopped

½ teaspoon ground turmeric

1 teaspoon ground coriander

½ teaspoon salt, plus extra for sprinkling

1–2 tablespoons lemon or lime juice

To Serve:

4 tablespoons plain yoghurt

garam masala, for sprinkling

2 tablespoons chopped fresh coriander leaves

Serves 4

Cut the aubergines in half lengthways and, using a spoon, scoop out the flesh leaving a 5 mm shell. Cube the flesh into 1.5 cm dice. Sprinkle the inside of the aubergine shells with salt and place in a colander, cut side down. Spread the aubergine cubes on a plate or tray or in a colander and sprinkle with more salt. Leave for about 30 minutes, then rinse well and pat dry with kitchen paper. Bring a pan of lightly salted water to the boil, add the potato cubes and cook for 5 minutes. Drain well and let cool. Place the aubergine shells, cut side up, on a baking sheet, brush with 2 tablespoons of the oil and cook in a preheated oven 190°C (375°F) Gas Mark 5 for 10–15 minutes until softened.

Remove from the oven and turn the aubergine shells upside down on a plate to drain off any excess oil.

Heat another 2 tablespoons of the oil in a large frying pan, add the cumin, mustard and sesame seeds and when they start to pop add the onion, garlic, ginger and chilli. Stir-fry for about 2–3 minutes then add the aubergine cubes. Cook, stirring occasionally, for 4–5 minutes or until they are just cooked, adding more oil as needed.

Stir in the turmeric, ground coriander and salt, then add the potatoes and stir-fry for 5–6 minutes until the potatoes are golden. Remove from the heat and stir in the lemon or lime juice. Taste and adjust the seasoning.

Put the aubergines back on the baking sheet, cut side up. Divide the potato mixture evenly between them and return to the oven for 10 minutes to heat through. Serve with the yoghurt and sprinkle with a little garam masala and the chopped fresh coriander.

Dhaal baht (rice and lentils) is a staple meal for millions of Indians and Nepalis. In this recipe, potatoes (*aloo*) are added to that traditional duo, and they are particularly desirable for their ability to absorb the wonderful flavours of Indian spices.

dhaal aloo

Indian potato curry
with toor dhaal (yellow lentils)

Wash the lentils well in several changes of water. Heat the oil in a large saucepan, over a low heat. Add the mustard and fenugreek seeds. When they begin to pop, stir in the ginger and garlic and fry for 30 seconds. Add the chilli powder, ground coriander and turmeric and stir-fry for a further 30 seconds. Add the tomatoes and lentils to the pan, cover with 600 ml water, add the salt, bring to the boil, reduce the heat, cover and simmer for 20–30 minutes or until the dhaal are just soft. Add the potatoes and simmer over a low heat for 10–15 minutes or until tender. Taste and adjust the seasoning. Sprinkle with chopped coriander and garam masala, add sprigs of fresh coriander and serve. Basmati rice and naan bread make suitable accompaniments.

125 g toor dhaal (yellow lentils)

3 tablespoons oil

½ teaspoon mustard seeds

½ teaspoon fenugreek seeds

1 teaspoon grated fresh ginger

1 teaspoon crushed garlic

1 teaspoon chilli powder

1½ teaspoons ground coriander

½ teaspoon ground turmeric

4 tomatoes, skinned and chopped

1 teaspoon salt

750 g floury potatoes, peeled and diced

2 tablespoons chopped fresh coriander,

plus extra sprigs, to serve

½ teaspoon garam masala, to serve

Serves 4

Australia and New Zealand have many unique varieties of potatoes, adapted to their wide range of climates. Antipodean chefs are brilliantly innovative, blending **European and Asian** traditions, and keen to work with **new and unusual** varieties of all kinds of foods.

australia
and new zealand

thai-style fish fingers
with frothy lime and lemongrass hollandaise

This dish is a perfect example of the eclectic influences found in Antipodean cooking. Australia's first settlers were British, followed the Chinese who came during the nineteenth-century Gold Rushes, then by Post-War migrants from Central and Southern Europe. Their most recent immigrants are from the Middle East and all over South-east Asia. The result is an exciting culinary mix, generally known as Pacific Rim or 'Fusion Food'.

This recipe is a South-east Asian twist on an old-fashioned English food, the hilariously named 'fish finger', with a classic French hollandaise plus Asian flavourings.

25 g unsalted butter

6 spring onions, finely chopped

I garlic clove, crushed

2.5 cm piece of fresh ginger,
peeled and finely grated

I red chilli, deseeded and
finely chopped

200 g fresh white crabmeat

2 tablespoons chopped fresh
coriander leaves

I teaspoon Thai fish sauce (*nam pla*)

250 g cooked floury potato, mashed

I egg, separated

25 g fresh breadcrumbs

25 g unsweetened desiccated coconut

salt and freshly ground black pepper

butter or sunflower oil, for frying

Lime and Lemongrass Hollandaise:

375 g unsalted butter

3 stalks lemongrass, chopped

3 tablespoons freshly
squeezed lime juice

finely grated zest of I lime
(preferably kaffir lime)

I teaspoon white peppercorns,
lightly crushed

I shallot, finely chopped

3 eggs, separated

Serves 4

To make the hollandaise, gently heat the butter and lemongrass in a small saucepan until the butter has melted. Remove from the heat, cover and set aside for 2–3 hours. (Keep it in a warm place so it doesn't solidify.)

To make the fish fingers, melt the 2 tablespoons butter in a pan, add the spring onions, garlic, ginger and chilli, cook gently for 5 minutes until softened, then transfer to a bowl and stir in the crab, coriander and fish sauce. Add the potato and beaten egg yolk and mix well to combine. Season to taste with salt and pepper

Divide the mixture into 12 pieces and form each into a rectangle 2.5 x 10 cm. Beat the egg white lightly with a fork, mix the breadcrumbs and coconut together and place in separate shallow bowls. Coat each fish finger in the egg white and then coat evenly in the crumb mixture. Set aside on a tray until ready to cook.

Heat a little butter or oil in a frying pan and cook the fish fingers in batches, for 3–4 minutes or until golden brown all over, then transfer to a baking sheet and keep them warm while you complete the hollandaise.

Put 2 tablespoons of the lime juice, 2 tablespoons water, lime zest, peppercorns and shallot in a small pan and boil until reduced to I tablespoon. While still warm, strain through a fine sieve into a bowl set over a pan of hot but not boiling water.

Add the egg yolks and beat well with a whisk. Continue whisking and add the butter in a thin steady stream (leaving the sediment and lemongrass pieces in the bottom of the pan) until all the clarified butter has been added and the hollandaise is thick and glossy. If it is very thick, whisk in a spoonful of hot water. Season to taste with salt, pepper and more lime juice if needed and remove from the heat.

In a separate bowl, whisk the egg whites until stiff but not dry. Stir one-third of the egg white into the hollandaise, then carefully fold in the rest.

Serve immediately with the fish fingers.

Many Australian immigrants still follow their family cooking traditions. Maria, the mother of my great friend Pina, left Calabria in Southern Italy for Melbourne 35 years ago. She still dries her own tomatoes, setting them on wicker trays on the garage roof covered with net curtains to ward off the flies. This recipe is a fine example of how the ingredients of one culture are absorbed into another.

potato mussel soup
with Italian sun-dried tomatoes

1 pinch of saffron strands
125 ml boiling water
175 ml dry white wine
1 kg mussels, scrubbed, debearded, broken or open ones discarded
fish or chicken stock (see method)
2 tablespoons olive oil
1 onion, sliced
1–2 cloves garlic, crushed
2.5 cm fresh ginger, peeled and finely grated
500 g potatoes, cut into 2.5 cm cubes
250 g tomatoes, skinned and chopped
8–10 sun-dried tomatoes, finely chopped
grated zest and juice of 1 orange
a sprig of thyme
salt and pepper
chopped fresh flat-leaf parsley, to serve

Serves 4

Put the saffron in a small heatproof bowl, pour over the boiling water and set aside to infuse. Pour the white wine into a pan large enough to accommodate all the mussels. Bring to the boil, add the mussels, cover with a tight-fitting lid and cook, shaking the pan frequently, for 2–3 minutes until the mussels have opened.

Tip the mussels into a colander set over a bowl, discarding any that have not opened. Remove two-thirds of the mussels from their shells and strain the mussel liquid through a muslin-lined sieve or coffee filter paper into a jug. Measure the liquid and make up to 900 ml with fish or chicken stock or water. Set aside.

Heat the olive oil in a large saucepan, add the onion, garlic and ginger and cook for 5–10 minutes until softened and translucent. Add the potatoes, tomatoes, sun-dried tomatoes and orange zest and cook for 1–2 minutes more. Add the reserved stock, the thyme, saffron and saffron soaking liquid, bring to the boil, reduce the heat and simmer for 15 minutes until the potatoes are tender. Add the orange juice and all of the mussels. Reheat and serve sprinkled with the chopped parsley.

This unusual combination of pasta and potatoes comes from an Italian-Australian friend whose family came from Genoa – and it is gorgeous! Though not traditional, it is characteristic of the exciting 'Fusion Food' found in Australia. I have dressed it with a wonderfully oily pesto of macadamia nuts. Macadamias are native to tropical Australia, where they are known as 'Queensland nuts'. They have a wonderful creamy texture, perfect for making sauces.

pasta and potatoes
with macadamia pesto

To make the pesto, place the basil, macadamia nuts and garlic in a blender or food processor and process until finely chopped. With the motor running, gradually add the oil in a thin stream until amalgamated. Scrape into a bowl, stir in the Parmesan and season to taste with salt and pepper.

Bring a pan of lightly salted water to a boil, add the potatoes and cook for 10–15 minutes, or until just tender. Drain and cool slightly, then peel and slice into 5 mm slices.

Cook the pasta in a large pan of boiling salted water according to the packet instructions. Drain in a colander but leave 2–3 tablespoons of the cooking water in the bottom of the pan. (A small amount of cooking water will help the sauce to amalgamate and cling to the pasta.)

Return the pasta to the pan, add the potato slices and half of the pesto and mix well. (Refrigerate the remaining pesto to use in another dish, such as the pesto mash on page 9.) Taste and adjust the seasoning and serve immediately with extra Parmesan cheese if preferred.

500 g new or salad potatoes
500 g tagliatelle
Macadamia Pesto:
50 g fresh basil leaves
75 g unsalted macadamia nuts, coarsely chopped
2 garlic cloves, chopped
175 ml extra-virgin olive oil
50 g Parmesan cheese, finely grated, plus extra to serve (optional)
salt and freshly ground black pepper
Serves 4

An extravagant dish of potatoes simmered gently in olive oil to melting tenderness. The oil can also be flavoured with garlic cloves or rosemary sprigs. This recipe is good with baked or barbecued fish – Australians are passionate about fish, and salmon is now farmed in the chilly southern waters off the island state of Tasmania.

confit of potatoes
with pan-roasted salmon

1 red pepper

1 yellow pepper

3 tomatoes, skinned, deseeded and chopped

1 tablespoon chopped fresh chives

1 litre good-quality extra-virgin olive oil*

750 g medium waxy potatoes, peeled and cut into even 5 mm slices

4 salmon fillets, 200–250 g each, seasoned on both sides

salt and freshly ground black pepper

Serves 4

*Though this quantity of oil may seem extravagant, it can be strained after cooking and re-used.

Cook the peppers on a baking sheet under a preheated grill for 15–20 minutes, turning occasionally, until charred and blistered all over. Put in a plastic bag, tie the top and let cool (the steam makes them easy to peel). When cool, peel and core the peppers, cut the flesh into small dice and put in a bowl with the tomatoes, chives, salt and pepper. Set aside.

Pour the oil into a saucepan, add the potatoes and bring to a very slow boil. When tiny bubbles rise to the surface, reduce the heat to very low and cook for 10 minutes. Test with the tip of a knife – the potatoes are cooked when they are still slightly firm in the centre. (This is a crucial stage: the potatoes continue cooking when removed from the heat, and if over-cooked they will become an oily mush.) Remove from the heat and keep them warm in the oil.

Heat 1 tablespoon of the oil in a large ovenproof frying pan over a moderate heat. Put the fish in the pan, skin side down, and cook for 2–3 minutes until the skin is crispy and golden. Turn the pieces over and cook in a preheated oven at 200°C (400°F) Gas Mark 6 for 5–6 minutes or until just cooked. Carefully remove the potato slices with a slotted metal spoon, drain well, then divide between 4 plates. Put a salmon fillet on top, surround with the peppers and tomatoes, then serve.

straw potato pancakes
with barbecued duck breasts

The use of pomegranates in this dish reflects the contribution made to the multi-cultural Australian cuisine by immigrants from the Middle East, especially from the Lebanon and Syria. Pomegranates are an important ingredient in Islamic cuisines, from Persia to Moghul India, the countries of Asia Minor and across North Africa. Their brilliant colour and sweet-sour taste are an excellent complement to the richness of duck. The crispy straw pancakes make a crunchy accompaniment to other meats, and like many potato dishes they sop up juices and gravies very well indeed.

3 pomegranates, halved
rind of 1 preserved lemon, chopped
1 garlic clove, crushed
2.5 cm piece of fresh ginger, peeled and finely grated
4 small duck breasts
500 g waxy potatoes
2 tablespoons clarified butter, plus extra if needed
1 tablespoon hazelnut oil
2 tablespoons honey
50 g roasted hazelnuts, chopped
a few salad leaves
salt and pepper
Serves 4

1 Scoop out the pomegranate seeds, discarding the white pith. Reserve 3 tablespoons of seeds, cover and chill. To make the marinade, put the remaining seeds in a blender and process briefly to release the juice.

2 Strain through a fine sieve into a flat non-metallic dish. Stir in the lemon zest, garlic and ginger. Score the skin of the duck 3–4 times and put in the marinade. Turn to coat, cover and chill for 12–24 hours, turning occasionally.

3 With a mandolin or sharp knife, cut the potatoes into thin julienne strips and put in cold water. Drain and rinse the potatoes 2–3 times to remove the starch. Drain, then dry well on a clean cloth. Put in a bowl and season well.

4 Heat the butter and oil in a large pan. Add spoonfuls of the potato to make 4 little cakes. Press down slightly and cook for 8–10 minutes, turn over and cook for 5–6 minutes more. Lift out of the pan and keep them warm.

5 Lift the duck from the marinade, pat dry and place on a preheated grill pan or barbecue. Cook, skin side down for 5 minutes, turn and cook 5 minutes more until tender, but still pink. Set aside to rest for 5 minutes. Slice thinly.

6 Bring the marinade and honey to the boil in a small pan and reduce until thickened. Season to taste. To serve, put a pancake on each plate, top with duck and pomegranate seeds, then add sauce, chopped nuts and salad leaves.

Here is an extravagant Antipodean version of the traditional British comfort food, 'bangers and mash' (sausages and mashed potatoes). The poaching sauce for the sausages makes use of the great sparkling wines produced in Australia.

bangers and mash
champagne sausages with chestnut potato purée

25 g unsalted butter

2 ripe pears

juice of 1 lemon

8 good-quality sausages

2 tablespoons soft brown sugar

400 ml champagne
or good sparkling wine

Chestnut Potato Purée:

375 g fresh chestnuts (cut a slash in
the pointed end of each one),
or 250 g vacuum-packed chestnuts

1 small Florence fennel bulb,
halved lengthways, cored and
roughly chopped

125 ml milk

125 ml double cream

1 kg floury potatoes,
unpeeled but well scrubbed

75 g unsalted butter

salt and freshly ground black pepper

Serves 4

If using fresh chestnuts to make the purée, put them in a pan, cover with cold water, bring to the boil and simmer for 2 minutes. Remove the pan from the heat. Using a slotted spoon, remove chestnut at a time and, using a small, sharp knife, remove the outer and inner skins. If the skins are difficult to peel, return the pan to the heat, return to the boil and simmer for 2 minutes more.

Put the chestnuts in a small pan with the fennel, milk and cream, bring to just below boiling, reduce the heat and simmer gently for 30–40 minutes if using fresh chestnuts (15–20 minutes if using vacuum-packed), or until tender. Strain and reserve the liquid. Purée the chestnuts and fennel in a food processor until smooth, spoon into a bowl, season to taste and set aside. Put the potatoes in cold water, bring to the boil and simmer for 15–20 minutes until tender. Drain, peel and press through a mouli, potato ricer or sieve, then add the chestnut mixture.

Peel the pears and cut in half lengthways and scoop out the core. Cut each half into 6 slices, dropping into a bowl of water acidulated with lemon juice to prevent discolouration. Drain well and pat dry on kitchen paper. Melt 15 g of the butter in a frying pan, add the pear slices and cook for about 4–5 minutes or until lightly golden. Remove with a slotted spoon and set aside.

Add the remaining butter to the pan, add the sausages and cook for 10 minutes until lightly golden. Add the sugar and wine, raise the heat to high and boil for 2–3 minutes or until reduced by half. Add the sliced pears and heat through. Place the chestnut potato purée in a pan, stir in the 75 g butter and reserved milk and cream mixture and reheat, stirring to prevent sticking. Season to taste. Serve the sausages on top the purée, then add the pears and sauce.

Tamarillos or tree tomatoes are a sub-tropical fruit, slightly soft when ripe, which can be eaten whole except for the skin. They are common in New Zealand gardens, and are often found in bigger supermarkets in other parts of the world. If unavailable, substitute plums or even apricots.

potato-crust lamb
with poached tamarillos

750 g waxy potatoes, peeled
1 garlic clove, crushed
2 tablespoons chopped fresh chives
2 tablespoons chopped fresh parsley
1 tablespoon fresh thyme leaves, removed from stalk
2 large egg yolks, beaten
12 lamb cutlets, very well trimmed, with all fat removed and the bone scraped clean
3 tablespoons olive oil
salt and pepper
sprigs of thyme, to serve

Poached Tamarillos:
6 tamarillos
150 ml port or red wine
150 ml lamb or chicken stock
3 tablespoons honey
5 cm cinnamon stick
½ teaspoon crushed coriander seeds
a piece of orange zest

Serves 4

Grate the potatoes finely and do not rinse. Put in a clean cloth and squeeze to extract any excess liquid. Put the grated potato in a bowl and add the garlic, herbs and egg yolks. Season with salt and pepper and mix well. Divide into 12 and wrap each lamb cutlet completely with the mixture.

To prepare the tamarillos, cut a small cross at the pointed end of each one with a sharp knife. Bring a pan of water to the boil, drop in the tamarillos and blanch for 30 seconds. Lift out with a slotted spoon and plunge into cold water. To make the sauce, carefully peel all the tamarillos, and finely chop 2 of them.

Put the port or red wine, stock, honey, cinnamon, crushed coriander seeds, orange zest and the chopped tamarillo in a shallow pan. Bring to the boil, reduce the heat, add the whole tamarillos and simmer for 3–4 minutes. Lift the fruit out of the sauce and set aside. Increase the heat and boil rapidly for about 2–3 minutes or until well reduced.

Heat the oil over a moderate heat in two large heavy-based frying pans. Add the lamb cutlets and cook for 3–4 minutes on each side or until the potato is tender and crispy and the lamb still pink. Slice the tamarillos, but leave them attached at the stalk, then place back into the sauce and reheat gently.

To serve, put 3 cutlets and 1 whole tamarillo on each plate. Drizzle over a little sauce and sprinkle with sprigs of thyme.

planning potato menus

Soups

Gingered seafood chowder with red roe cream and poppyseed crackers 18

Potage parmentier with parsley oil and croûtons 44

Potato mussel soup with Italian sun-dried tomatoes 128

Potato peanut soup with deep-fried plantain strips 102

Salads and Snacks

Blue potato salad 17

Empanaditas 24

Malaysian popiah 115

Mini potato roti with coconut and mint chutney 108

Potato chap 94

Potato pakoras with spicy tomato chutney 106

Roasted warm potato salad 17

Sultan's salad 91

Vegetable samosas with potato and cauliflower 110

Fish and Seafood

Confit of potatoes with pan-roasted salmon 133

Crispy potato tostadas with salmon and scallop seviche 16

Fish and chips: tuna strips with potato ribbons 42

Portuguese salt cod fritters with Greek skorthalia 68

Potato pancakes with mackerel gravad lax 47

Thai-style fish fingers with frothy lime and lemongrass hollandaise 126

Poultry

Chicken pot pie with porcini mushrooms and potato pastry 34

Chicken potato stew with 'Seville' oranges 92

Potato turnovers with chicken livers 66

Straw potato pancakes with barbecued duck breasts 134

Thai chicken curry with potatoes and coconut milk 116

Meat

Champagne sausages with chestnut potato purée 138

Moroccan couscous 100

Potato-crust lamb with poached tamarillos 140

Tortitas de papa with chorizo and corn salsa verde 33

One-dish Meals

American baked potato with fluffy soufflé fillings 29

Indian dry potato curry in aubergine shells with yoghurt 121

Indian potato curry with toor dhaal yellow lentils 122

Kuku sibzamini 90

Potato gratin with herbs, spinach and cheese 61

Potato soufflé with mozzarella and almond-parsley pesto 62

Vegetable Accompaniments

Bay-roasted hasselbacks 72

Cajun potato wedges with spicy lemon and onions 37

Champ 74

Clapshot 74

Colcannon 74

Cracked new potatoes in coriander and red wine 59

Hash browns 38

Jansson's temptation 71

Pommes voisin 81

Potatoes dauphinoise 76

Potatoes en papillote scented with fresh herbs 22

Punchnep 74

Rumbledethumps 74

Swiss rösti 54

Pastry and Pasta

Chilli potato tart with roasted tomatoes and garlic 30

Pasta and potatoes with macadamia pesto 130

Pizza con le patate 52

Potato gnocchi with walnut and rocket pesto 48

Baking and Sweet Things

Golden potato scones with parmesan and pancetta 86

Honey potato bread with saffron and a poppyseed glaze 85

Potato noodles with red cherry compote 82

index

author's acknowledgements

I would like to thank the many people
who gave their advice, help and assistance
to me in the writing of this book. They
include:

Jennifer John and Hazel Jenkins,
British Potato Council,
Broad Field House, 4 Between Towns
Road Oxford, OX4 3NA
Tel 01865 714455, Fax 01865 782 254

Wendy Jenkins,
The National Potato Promotion Board
7555 E. Hampton Avenue, No. 412
Denver, Colorado 80231
Tel 303.369.7718, Fax 303.369.7718

John, Duncan and Martin and staff at:
Panzers Fruit and Vegetables
13–19 Circus Road
St John's Wood, London, NW8
Tel. 0171 722 8162

Many organic thanks to Julian Turner for
his fabulous Edzell blues and his friend
Mr Nicholson for his Shetland Blacks.

Chris, Jerry and Richard
Frank Godfrey Ltd
7 Highbury Park, London. N5 1QJ
Tel. 0171 226 2425

Richard Bartlett for his wonderful and
unusual specialist salad leaves
Halcyon Herbs
10 Hampden Close, Chalgrove,
Oxfordshire OX44 7SB
Tel 01865 890180

For information on rare and unusual
potatoes or other vegetable varieties,
contact the organically excellent:
Henry Doubleday Research Association
Ryton Organic Gardens
Coventry CV8 3 LG
Tel 01203 303 517Fax 01203 639229
Email: enquiry@hdra.org.uk
World Wide Web: http://www.hdra.org.uk